PRAISE FOR

A Healing Place

"As an adult who lost both my mom and dad at a young age, *A Healing Place* really speaks to my soul. Kate Atwood finally gives a voice to all kids struggling to survive and thrive after their parent's death. I only wish her wisdom would have been available to my family...what a profound difference it could have made in all of our lives. Kate's advice made me laugh and cry and serves as a great reminder that the journey to heal is never ending."

— Jennifer Bernstein Adams, executive producer for CNN

"Kate Atwood is living what I call an 'inside-out' story. She's taken the devastating loss of her mother at a young age and turned the experience inside out. She's transformed her life and the world of many children with Kate's Club, and now she promises to transform countless others with this book, written from love, wisdom and experience. Kate is an inspiration to anyone who has ever faced loss and tragedy. She truly shows what's possible!"

— Daryn Kagan, creator and host of DarynKagan.com

"Kate has been a wonderful inspiration to my children and me. The connection that comes from this shared experience is magical, and focusing on the love and influence of the person we lost, rather than the tragedy of the loss itself, is life changing."

— Andi, Alec and Adam Stein
In loving memory of Paul Stein

A
Healing
Place

Help Your Child Find
Hope and Happiness
After the Loss of a Loved One

KATE ATWOOD

WITH JOHN KELLY

A PERIGEE BOOK

A PERIGEE BOOK
Published by the Penguin Group
Penguin Group (USA) Inc.
375 Hudson Street, New York, New York 10014, USA

Penguin Group (Canada), 90 Eglinton Avenue East, Suite 700, Toronto, Ontario M4P 2Y3, Canada
(a division of Pearson Penguin Canada Inc.)
Penguin Books Ltd., 80 Strand, London WC2R 0RL, England
Penguin Group Ireland, 25 St. Stephen's Green, Dublin 2, Ireland (a division of Penguin Books Ltd.)
Penguin Group (Australia), 250 Camberwell Road, Camberwell, Victoria 3124, Australia
(a division of Pearson Australia Group Pty. Ltd.)
Penguin Books India Pvt. Ltd., 11 Community Centre, Panchsheel Park, New Delhi—110 017, India
Penguin Group (NZ), 67 Apollo Drive, Rosedale, North Shore 0632, New Zealand
(a division of Pearson New Zealand Ltd.)
Penguin Books (South Africa) (Pty.) Ltd., 24 Sturdee Avenue, Rosebank, Johannesburg 2196,
South Africa
Penguin Books Ltd., Registered Offices: 80 Strand, London WC2R 0RL, England

While the author has made every effort to provide accurate telephone numbers and Internet addresses at the time of publication, neither the publisher nor the author assumes any responsibility for errors, or for changes that occur after publication. Further, the publisher does not have any control over and does not assume any responsibility for author or third-party websites or their content.

Copyright © 2009 by Kate Atwood
Cover art by Corbis
Cover design by Wendy Bass
Text design by Kristin del Rosario

First edition: October 2009

Library of Congress Cataloging-in-Publication Data

Atwood, Kate.
A healing place : help your child find hope and happiness after the loss of a loved one / Kate Atwood with John Kelly.
    p.   cm.
ISBN 978-0-399-53504-8
1. Bereavement.   2. Children and death.   I. Kelly, John.   II. Title.
BF575.G7.A896 2009
155.9'37—dc22   2009022953

PRINTED IN THE UNITED STATES OF AMERICA

10 9 8 7 6 5 4 3 2 1

This book describes the real experiences of real people. The author has disguised the identities of some, and in some instances created composite characters, but none of these changes has affected the truthfulness and accuracy of her story. Penguin is committed to publishing works of quality and integrity. In that spirit, we are proud to offer this book to our readers; however, the story, the experiences and the words are the author's alone.

Most Perigee books are available at special quantity discounts for bulk purchases for sales promotions, premiums, fund-raising, or educational use. Special books, or book excerpts, can also be created to fit specific needs. For details, write: Special Markets, Penguin Group (USA) Inc., 375 Hudson Street, New York, New York 10014.

To the kids at Kate's Club, who inspire me every day to live life to the fullest.

ACKNOWLEDGMENTS

One of life's most precious gifts is people who believe in *you*! I'm fortunate to be surrounded by many wonderful people who have believed in me through both struggles and successes. This book would not be possible without all of those believers.

Thank you to my mom, who in twelve short years taught me all about sharing with others, from toys to love, compassion, and grief. To my dad, whose support has empowered me to be the best at everything I set out to do in life. To both my dad and brother, who have been on this crazy journey with me since April 25, 1991. You are two of the most amazing, wonderful men in the world, and I love you every minute of every day.

To Bebe, Margaret, and Charles—you all have been a great support and I'm honored to have you as family.

To my extended family who have supported me in my grief and in my life. Your love has filled my heart in times when it felt so hollow.

To my dearest friends without whom I would not be the woman I am today. You have taught me lessons and love that would otherwise have been missed had I not had you *all* in my life. To Lily, Vanessa, Yasmin, Jules, Cali, Ashley, Carrie, Brynee and Ansley, with whom I have shed the most tears and shared the most laughs, your unwavering support through all of these years has been nothing short of angelic.

To my heroic mentors, Daryn Kagan, Will Marré, Kristi Atkins and Melinda Chandler who have always believed in my professional ambition and continue to encourage me to always strive for a higher level of success.

To John Kelly, for believing in this project and helping me put beautiful, organized prose to my passionate and somewhat chaotic thoughts. To Maria Gagliano, my editor, for being the most gracious, empowering, and constructive critic. I have enjoyed working with both of you through this entire process.

To Lynne Hughes who gave me my voice to tell my story for this first time. With the power of this voice, I got to meet the Steins, Habberfields and Jacksons—the first families of Kate's Club. And to Ron Clark who grew my voice through an endorsement that led to the opportunity to write this book.

I often am the person who receives praise for the work of Kate's Club, but it is undeniably more appropriate to be given to the staff and volunteers of Kate's Club. I feel lucky to work with such gifted, gracious and selfless individuals every day. This praise also must be shared with the board members at Kate's Club, who have helped to take Kate's Club to a level of success that I only dreamed of it reaching.

Most important, this book would not be possible without the kids and families of Kate's Club. Your courage and compassion are examples to us all.

CONTENTS

When I was twelve years old, there were two people I knew whose mother had died. Wait, make that three. There was Cinderella, Snow White and me. Great . . . twelve years old, looking for answers on how to navigate a reality I never could have imagined, and the only people I had to look to for support and understanding were two fairy tale princesses.

And that, more than anything else, is the reason I am writing this book.

It took me the better part of eight years to learn the most important lesson about grief: that *no one* should have to do it alone.

From the moment that lesson was revealed to me, on a magical evening at a bereavement camp for kids in Richmond, Virginia, I made it a life mission to share this message with as many people as possible. It is why I started Kate's Club, a nonprofit organization geared toward helping kids and families through the grief journey by encouraging them to go out and proactively live the lives and experience the joy they deserve. I now want to share my insights with all of you. Why? In continuing my growth and journey with grief as a part of my life, I have come to realize that the most important place for a child to feel safe to grieve is right at home.

Kate's Club's staff and volunteers work tirelessly to create a place for our kids and their families where it is OK to grieve. But Kate's Club is a healing place for kids in Atlanta. With this book, I will help you to create a healing place right in your home. Within these chapters I will provide you with some of the building blocks to create a healing place for your children after you and they have lost a loved one. Not only will I give you some broad tips to directly support your children, but I will also empower you to at times reach out for support as well.

I encourage you to read this book through and then come back to it whenever you may need a little boost of support during those times when grief seems a little more present and intense in your family. Though I don't know your individual story, the tips here are designed to help you further identify ways to help your child after the death of Mom or Dad.

I am not here to give you all the answers. I am here to

provide you with the inspiration to discover them. Each grief journey is different, but I believe in the incredible power of shared experiences to move us forward and lift us up. Even when it comes to something as devastating as loss—in fact, *especially* when it comes to something as devastating as loss.

Despite its great sadness, grief is also closely associated with the most important emotion any of us can ever feel. Because if there is one thing I've learned on my own journey it is that, stripped to its bare essentials, grief is love. We'll talk about it later in this book, but just think about it for a second. We grieve because we hurt. We hurt because we miss. We miss because we love. The pain that comes from grief, as brutal as it can be, emanates from a wellspring of love.

In these pages you'll find stories of people who are walking in your shoes. You'll find observations and opinions and suggestions. But most of all, my fondest wish is that you will find hope. We'll take a journey with the common goal of building a healing environment that will better allow your child to get the support he needs, from you and from other key people in his life.

We'll start with a broad understanding of grief in our culture and some of the common obstacles you will face. For instance, as you likely have already discovered, our American society generally isn't comfortable with death and dying. Next, we'll talk about how important it is to support yourself so that you can be available, strong and healthy enough to do the same for your kids. Once we have addressed your own grief, we'll move into the keys to supporting your kids: from communication to memories to laughter and beyond. Each of these elements plays a big role in laying the healing foundation for your home and lives. Finally we'll move through some ways to maintain these core philosophies as you continue on in life.

You'll always have difficult times and difficult inter-actions when it comes to your kids and their reaction to and understanding of grief. The holidays will always be tough. In fact, all milestones may have a sting to them now that Mom or Dad isn't there. Traditions will have to evolve so you can continue to experience hope and enjoyment from them. But I'm here to tell you that you can certainly celebrate all of these special times, in spite of grief. I know from my own life experiences and the ones I have shared with the families at Kate's Club that you and your children have so much hope and happiness ahead in your life. It's my goal to help you see and feel that for yourself.

It has never been my goal to master grief, nor should it be yours. Grief is incredibly dynamic and complex. It has garnered the career-long attention of psychological and sociological experts around the world. I am not a scientist. I am not a clinical expert in the field of counseling. There is nothing special about me other than the choice I made to try and help people understand that in grief they are deal-ing with not only an ending, but a beginning. And to help people understand that the positives of life are still right there within their reach.

I know because I've been there. I've learned how to find silver linings in what are usually the most traumatic experiences of anyone's life. That is why, when it comes to grief, I consider myself more of an *ambassador* than an expert.

What's the difference? An expert is someone who takes knowledge provided by others and relays findings. An ambassador is someone who simply takes knowledge of her own and gives it a voice that can empower others to take action. I am not here to say this is what you should or should not do. My job is to let people know that these are the opportunities available to them, that these are the paths they can follow.

As an ambassador, I feel very fortunate to share these journeys, and to be able to offer what I have learned to help others. Of all the things I've learned, there is one that stands out. Every grieving child, no matter the circumstances of the child's life and their loss, is seeking the same thing: the path of most hope.

From the day we opened our doors, hope has been a cornerstone of Kate's Club, and it is at the heart of our philosophy of helping kids process both grief and life. Hope is painted into the bold, bright colors of our clubhouse walls, colors put there in intentional defiance of our stilted cultural definition of grief. It is heard the minute you step inside and hear kids doing what kids do best, as they play, share, learn, laugh, cry and *live*. Kate's Club is about helping these children learn how to live lives that are colored by, but not defined by, their grief.

Before I ever truly understood or laid out the details of Kate's Club, I knew that it would be a place where hope would be valued and promoted above all else. I knew it would be a place where kids would feel comfortable celebrating life in the way all kids deserve to. In the early days of Kate's Club, it was just me, a handful of volunteers, and the kids riding around Atlanta in a rented minivan. We were in search of fun and adventures that would take the children away from life's new realities and put them in touch with peers who understood what they were going through like no one else could. What struck me right away was how easily these kids shared their stories, and themselves, with one another. It was like an instant community bond was formed. They were clearly in it together.

In those days we went to Atlanta Braves games, to the zoo . . . anyplace where they could experience the kind of joy that had been taken away from them. If you saw us in those days, grief would have been the last thing on your mind. And that was just as I intended it. And with one another these kids shared effortlessly the same stories that parents, family members and even trained professionals had probably been struggling to get out of them since their loss occurred.

Today Kate's Club has evolved into a multidimensional organization that serves hundreds of kids with a comprehensive range of events and services, from structured and non-structured social interaction to licensed therapy. Yet no matter how we have grown and will grow in the future, the core offering of Kate's Club will always be hope, and the key by-product of that hope will always be empowerment— empowerment brought forth by the simple exercise of letting kids be kids. That is one of the most important things to remember through this entire book. At a time that calls for them to grow up way too fast, letting your kids be kids will help them more than anything else to follow the best and healthiest path forward.

Hope is about understanding and accepting the uncertainty of a life touched by grief. Empowerment is what leads us to action. For me, that empowerment first came, and continues to come, from the seemingly simple exercise of telling my story. I first shared mine with a camp full of young kids who revealed to me a community I never really knew existed. By now I've shared the story thousands of times, with parents and families, in lecture halls, auditoriums and even with Rosie O'Donnell and a national television audience on *The View*. I'm amazed at how powerful the act of telling it remains for me to this day.

Now I want your child to feel that power that comes with owning that story and finding that voice. And I want to help you work with your child to create the healing place within not only your home, but other environments as well. This is the place you and your child deserve, and I look forward to helping you get there!

First Things First

One of the first things we must understand is that we can't make a child's grief go away. And we shouldn't try. What you need to do is work with your child to help him move through a new life with grief as a part of it.

Society's discomfort with death, loss and grief puts you squarely behind the eight ball. The anthropologist Margaret Mead had it right when she said, "When a person is born we rejoice, and when they're married we jubilate. But when they die we try to pretend nothing has happened." Most people would rather discuss anything but these topics. This makes your job harder, but even more crucial.

So let me start with a first tip. Ready? The most powerful tool for helping grieving kids is something we all have at our disposals at all times: one another.

My goal in starting Kate's Club was to create a literal healing place for kids. A place where they could go and be themselves, supported by peers and adults with a real understanding of what they were going through. A place where it was OK to cry, but also OK to laugh and, most important, to live. I am writing this book to provide you with tools and tips to help you create a healing place in your child's life. And that process has to start in the first place where healing begins—in your own home.

I've heard a lot of grief stories. And the healthiest ones of all come from those kids and adults who have made their home a true foundation. For them, it is a place of comfort and safety, of solid ground and shared strength. Once they have this strength, these people can go out into the rest of the world and find healing there too.

Building this foundation will be some of the hardest work you will do. It's so easy to take a passive approach, when what you really need is an active and inclusive one. This is the time for your family to establish the fact that you are going to get through this together. You might find strength to do this in your religion. You might find it in your family and friends. You might find it from your children themselves. But the point is you can find it, by openly acknowledging what you all are going through, with all the difficult emotions that go along with it. The fact that you are reading these words right now tells me you have already taken a huge step toward creating your new healthy, healing life. That open mind and open heart will serve you well.

Finding your healing place is your personal quest. No one can write you an architectural plan. What I will do here is give you building blocks that will help you design it for yourself. You are now on a shared journey and I am honored to spend this part of it with you. Each time I meet a new family at Kate's Club, I like to say, "I'm glad you're here." For my part, I would like to say I'm definitely glad *you're* here and I look forward to sharing your journey.

You bring something entirely unique to your journey. You bring your story. This will be an amazing tool that can give you peace and that can give strength to others.

I know mine did for me. So let me share it with you.

CHAPTER ONE

My Story

In the summer of 1999, my whole life changed with a simple tap on the shoulder.

I was twenty years old and between my junior and senior years of college—a crucial year for soon-to-be-graduates to find activities and connections that will help guide their future careers. I was all set to work for the summer at Public City School Day Camp in my hometown of Charlottesville, Virginia. I also made a decision to try an overnight camp located an hour away in Richmond called Camp Comfort, now named Comfort Zone Camp, which focused on helping children who were grieving the death of a loved one.

It was hardly the choice most people would make for an extracurricular activity, especially during their last unofficial summer of freedom. For me, though, it was a natural.

It represented the chance to make a connection that I had long been craving.

Eight years earlier, at the age of twelve, I had suffered the worst loss a child can imagine when my mother died after a six-year-battle with breast cancer.

My mom, Audrey Atwood, was unforgettable. And I say that not only from my own limited memories, or from my own bias. I say it because it has been supported by so many people who knew and loved her. I say it because it was true.

She was a tall, beautiful, striking woman, the kind of person who would walk into a room and, no matter whether it was filled by children or adults, grab attention by her very presence. She never tried to turn the focus on her, mind you, because she never had to.

She just had this unexplainable aura about her—a dynamic bundle of good energy that drew people to her. People likened her to a Princess Diana figure in our little town, not for any regal airs, but because she exuded compassion and sincerity and because she was so unquestionably genuine. My mom was the person whom people innately trusted and to whom people always came in times of need for the guidance and comfort that I still miss so dearly.

She was first diagnosed with breast cancer in 1985. She was thirty-five years old. She was diagnosed after discovering a lump in her breast and dutifully going to her doctor to have it checked out. Remember, breast cancer in the 1980s didn't carry near the clout with health professionals that it does today. Her first doctor quickly dismissed the tumor as benign and called for no further action to be taken. My mom was a fan of good news, and decided to forgo getting a second opinion. My dad and a few close friends pressed her on this point, and she finally relented to their wishes. As it turned out, it was this window of time between these two doctor visits that ultimately sealed her fate.

The second opinion included a biopsy of the lump that brought the worst possible news. The tumor was, in fact, malignant. She would battle the disease for the next six years, but in the end, it would get the best of her. She lost her life way too soon—for her as well as for me.

Almost immediately after my mom died, my life became a tireless quest to move forward without ever treading anywhere near the cavernous hole her loss had created in our lives. My brother, who was two years older, and father took similar yet separate roads. Our strategy was all we knew. The Atwoods were survivors, and we would, each in his or her own way, fight to avoid defeat, even in the face of these impossible challenges. It is a strategy I might have employed for the rest of my life, if not for that little hand that reached across so much fear and uncertainty in order to make a connection.

"You're Kate . . . Right?"

I had no idea what to expect the first day I pulled up at Camp Comfort (now called Comfort Zone Camp), where I didn't know a single soul. All I knew was that I felt pretty comfortable with the whole grief issue. I could help these kids. After all, I was already healed!

Yeah . . . riiiiiiiight.

I had been there a few hours when I was approached by the camp's founder, who asked if I would speak to the entire camp that night and share my story. She told me I was the youngest volunteer at the camp and that she felt like the kids would be able to relate well to me. She also explained to me that my role for the camp would be "junior buddy," as I had not completed the training the other volunteers had. Those volunteers, called "big buddies," were each assigned a specific kid for the entire weekend, while I was able to roam and provide support when needed. It gave me a great overview of the entire camp experience and prepared me well for the years to follow, when I would take on, and absolutely love, my big buddy role.

Now back to the story sharing part. I was excited about the opportunity because I've never been one to turn down a microphone! Yet telling my story, especially in a setting like this, was something I had never done before, so a little nervousness would have been understandable. Then why, when my name was called to come up to the front, did I feel none? I had not had time to even think about what I was going to say, let alone prepare a script. So I just took a deep breath and off I went . . .

Hi, my name is Kate Atwood and my mom died of cancer when I was twelve. She had breast cancer.

I can still remember focusing on the squeaky-clean

treads of a brand-new sneaker in the front row and the tiny fingers that were idly picking at it. For those first couple of minutes, I was speaking, but the voice inside my head was mute. I was doing exactly what an overwhelming majority of us do when faced with our own grief: I was mumbling through my story of loss for fear that, at best, what I was saying would be misinterpreted and, at worst, I would be seen as someone seeking pity. At this camp, though, on this night, pity was out the window, along with fear, shame and all of those other emotions that hold grieving kids back. Before long I realized that the eyes that had once stared downward were now locked on me, and that they were wide open, engaged and connecting. It was my first clue of the true power of shared experiences.

I had figured my story would last two or three minutes— that I would just throw the facts out there, maybe talk about how I was excited to be part of the whole thing and how much I looked forward to getting to know everybody. Instead, to my surprise, *they* were the ones getting to know *me*, in a way very few others had since my mom's death.

In a very surreal way, I could feel that this moment was bigger than I, and I just allowed myself to be in it. When it was over, I couldn't tell if I had been speaking for five minutes or for twenty-five. I don't remember all I said, but I do remember fading into the comfort of the release and just letting it all flow out through my voice.

Here I was in this social wilderness of total strangers, of all ages, talking about things I had never shared with my family or closest friends. This, I remember thinking, is what freedom feels like. I may not have realized it right away, but I had found that priceless tool that I had been most longing for since my mother's death. *I had found my voice.*

What happened later that night put an exclamation point on the experience, and changed the course of my life.

While I was brushing my teeth and getting ready for bed, I noticed in the mirror's reflection a little girl in her nightgown standing beside her big buddy. She looked hesitant to approach the sink next to me. As I bowed my head to rinse, I felt a little tap. I turned around to see this young, beautiful face before me.

"You're Kate?" the little voice said timidly, "You lost your mom, right?"

"Hi . . . Yes, she passed away when I was twleve."

The little girl must have been no more than nine or ten years old, with long, wavy brown hair and one of those faces that you just know will hold its beauty forever. Everything about her looks reflected the young girl she was, so innocent and curious. But she was composed in a way that many adults twenty years her senior are not. Continuing to focus on what she was going to tell me, I just leaned down and listened.

"Well, my mom and my dad . . . they died. They died in a car wreck and I live with my aunt and my uncle now. I have a sister and a brother. They are at camp too." Her tone was so matter-of-fact. So trusting.

I remember thinking, OK . . . what in the world am I supposed to say to that? Before I could answer that question for myself, I was already talking.

"Thank you so much for sharing that with me. I'm so glad you have your sister and brother in your life too." Where did those words even come from, and who was this person using them? I know now that they came from the empowerment I felt, from the connection we had made. We said our good nights, and the little girl who'd made the big difference headed off with her buddy.

Later that night, at the first counselor's meeting, one of the counselors stood up and introduced herself as Sarah's big buddy. She told everyone how Sarah's uncle had dropped the girl off at the camp that afternoon and had talked about his serious concerns about how she was handling the tragedy. She had been this incredibly dynamic young girl, and now that spark had completely disappeared from her eyes and her life. She had not, he said, ever spoken a word about her loss to anyone.

"I just wanted everyone to know," the buddy said, "that Sarah approached Kate in the bathroom tonight and shared her story."

As my peers in that meeting shared their congratulations with me, I was already beginning to process my interaction with Sarah. It was opening my eyes to things I had never seen before. Up until that night, my mother's death was the only single moment that had changed my life forever. Now, because of that moment, I was being given another moment that would change me in a completely different way. That moment gave me a purpose. It gave me a mission. It gave me perspective. And it gave me my future.

I've often wondered where I would be without that moment. I have long been thankful for the many opportunities it has offered me to help so many kids and families. But most important, that was the moment I realized that I was not alone in my grief and that I, just like you, had the power to help others along their grief journeys.

The Big "K"

I was six years old when my mother was diagnosed with breast cancer. Six years old, and the only thing I knew for sure about cancer was that it started with a "k."

My parents worked hard to protect my brother and me from the details of this horrible monster of a disease. I'm sure they had every confidence that my mom, such an extraordinary and strong woman, would beat it anyway. Yet, somehow, even at that young age, I had a sense that our life as a family would never be the same.

But my parents did an incredible thing. They allowed me to be a kid. I was a good one at times, a brat at others, and one who, I have heard, had a unique ability to make my mom's eyes shine. She got to nurture me, to teach me, to mold me, to love me and, as only moms can do to pre-adolescent girls, to embarrass me.

She just didn't get to do any of it for long enough.

I am amazed when I think of how hard it must have been to preserve and protect my brother's and my experiences as children. This was a woman who was fiercely devoted, even as her illness progressed and then overtook her, to making sure that we understood that life was there for the celebrating.

I knew that something was different with my mother. There were the treatments, the random nights that my brother and I would have to spend away from home. None of it really registered though, even right down to the end, when she was in a hospital bed at home, on oxygen, receiving regular nursing care and making frequent trips back and forth to the hospital. What was actually happening was just too far out of the realm of possibility for me to even consider. I mean, come on. That just doesn't happen. Your mom can't *die*. In fact, I was so sure of this that one day I told her. We were in the car and she was telling me that a friend of mine's father had committed suicide.

"That's not right," I said. "Parents don't die." I've often thought about how heartbreaking that moment must have been for her. I'd love to have those three words back.

April 25, 1991: The Unimaginable

One night in April of 1991 I came home from a softball game and walked into the room where my mom had been staying during what I now know was her in-home hospice care. The bed was all made up, the room oddly still and silent. My grandmother came in and I immediately turned and said, "Where's my mom?"

She said, "She was having some trouble breathing and we were just wanting to be sure, so we called the ambulance." I had no idea that this was the inevitable reality everyone else had been waiting for. The bed, the machines, the nurses . . . it was all a setup for the end, the one my mother wanted, peaceful and at home. For weeks I had been coming home and spending time with her, lying in that narrow bed and sharing the day's events. Despite the assisted breathing machines, the constant nurse visits . . . the fear of loss had never even entered my mind.

"OK," I said. "Where's my dad?"

My grandmother told me he was going to stay with my mom at the hospital for the night and not to worry about anything. So I went about the rest of my night, as if nothing was terribly wrong. Denial carried me into the morning, through my usual before-school routine. It lasted me the ride into school and the usual small talk with friends. It lasted me, in fact, until mid-morning.

I was sitting in Mrs. Kerewich's Social Studies class and there was a call over the intercom. "Kate Atwood, please report to the office, and bring your things." As I look back, this was a classic example of just how fearful we as a society are of death and grief, particularly when it comes to young people. I mean, seriously . . . the *intercom*? Who in the world would not think to come and get a child in that situation, to remove her from the classroom in a quieter, gentler and more personal way?

I have used this scenario in presentations to guidance counselors and school administrators as an example of how we as adults must wiggle out of our own comfort zones to tend to the comfort of the grieving child. It still breaks me today.

I had been working on a project with my friend Kyle and I looked at him, and looked at my teacher, who said, "OK, Kate, get your stuff." She thought nothing odd of it. I did.

I turned to Kyle and said, "It's my mom. I'm not going."

I don't know how long I stood there. The next thing I knew I saw a guidance counselor and my grandfather in the doorway of the classroom.

We walked outside, and I got into a waiting van, driven by my dad's best friend, Jim. My grandfather got into the front seat and my brother was beside me in the back. My brother just glanced at me and quickly glanced away. He had definitely been crying.

The van pulled away in total silence.

In my mind, my mom was already dead. So when we arrived at the hospital, Chris, a nurse at the hospital who was also my mom's best friend, wrapped me in a hug and then asked if I wanted to go see her, I said, "Oh. She's still alive?" This really confused me. I was thinking, OK, so if she is actually alive, what am I even doing here?

We walked to her room, and the whole thing was still not registering with me. I knew one thing. I knew I did not want any part of going into that room to see her. Something in me told me that if I did, nothing would ever be the same again. I watched as my brother walked right in and so naturally and gracefully took a seat by her side. It took a gentle push from my father to get me to follow.

The first thing I noticed was the terrible and foreign sound of her breathing. It was what is commonly known as the death rattle. She was in a coma and her lungs were filling with fluid. She was fighting for each and every breath. I'll never hear a worse sound.

I finally got the courage to sit by her bed, and I began whispering to her. I told her about all my fears of losing her, of not having her there for my prom, for my wedding day, for all the major life events to come. It was such a typical child's response, focusing only on myself, on the only level of emotional understanding I could come up with. The irony is that here I was talking about all these great big life moments, with no clue that it would ultimately be the millions of smaller moments that would bring me to my knees.

My brother never left my mom's side that day. As for me, I needed protection, and that was my dad's specialty. I stuck to him like glue. Of course, I had no idea that he had been up with my mom all night long. So when he decided to duck into the lounge and take a nap, I decided I would do the same thing.

We actually did fall asleep for a bit before we were gently awoken by Chris. She told us my mom had taken her last breath. My dad turned to me as I lay there still desperately trying to fight off the reality that this tiny nap had staved off for a few moments. He said, "It's all over."

At that point, we began to walk back toward the room. I remember somebody telling me that my mother was now at peace, whatever that was supposed to mean to a twelve-year-old at that moment.

There I stood in that doorway again, and if I had been hesitant about going in before, I was now trying to permanently root myself in the floor. I stood, absolutely drowning in tears, until I was literally pushed into the room. They wanted me to say good-bye. How in the world was I supposed to do *that*? I just stood there for a while longer. Finally, I watched as some people from the hospital entered the room and took her away.

Reality on that day and those that followed came in powerful life snapshots, and I experienced one later that night. It was a moment that signaled the beginning of a new phase of our lives, and one that proved how little we knew about how to handle any of it.

I walked into my parents' room and there was my father, lying (very symbolically) on my mother's side of their bed. He was crying. And for me, seeing my dad cry was a first. He is and will always be about moving forward, about picking yourself up from any fall and steamrolling right ahead.

But even as my father lay there crying, I couldn't, or

wouldn't, recognize his grief. "I think," I said, "that I am in shock." It seemed so odd to me. This just didn't make sense. How could I be in a good mood?

He answered that I was not, in fact, in shock. That shock would be if she had been killed in a car wreck that day. I know now what he was trying to say. For him, this death was not a shock in that he had an adult's understanding of my mom's diagnosis and had been preparing for the inevitability of this moment. This was something I was incapable of understanding. But the fact remained that on that night, in that room, no word choice or different set of circumstances would have fixed the only thing that mattered.

My mom was gone and our lives had changed forever.

Keeping It Simple

Everyone reading this book is at a different point in his or her grief journey. Thus the tips included here will have different meanings for everyone. I think I can safely assume, however, that you have already had your initial conversations with your children about your mutual loss and the new life that lies ahead. Maybe you have experienced some frustration in these talks and can identify with the example I shared of the conversation between my father and me.

The important lesson here is that the exact details of what we were both going through did not matter. We were in our own worlds—mine as a child and his as an adult. And we were both trying to regain our footing there.

This is something you must keep in mind throughout your mutual journeys. Always remember that you are experiencing things on completely different emotional planes. You must try to bring yourself to that kid level in order to try and understand what he is feeling. It's kind of like kids and sarcasm. Many times, they just don't get it. Their minds are often not mature enough to understand adult humor. You are going through grief as an adult, with a more mature emotional scale and vocabulary to support what you are feeling. You need to help your child find the words and their expression, just as you did when she was learning her first words. If your child turns away from a conversation, it may not be because he is avoiding a tough topic, it may be because he is out of his emotional depth.

Let's take grief out of the equation for a second. Remember when your kids were growing up and you read them bedtime stories? Did you pick up *The Iliad* or *The Odyssey*? No, you probably started with *Goodnight Moon* or some book like it. You read what you knew your kids could understand and process.

So do the same thing when it comes to grief. Don't expect children to be able to fully understand, let alone verbally communicate with you about, how they are feeling. This takes time and effort on both your parts, often supplemented by outside support as well.

Take some extra time to consider how your child is experiencing these events and emotions. Meet her where she thinks and feels, and provide her comfort that way. This is a tall order, especially when you are processing your own grief, but it will do a world of good down the road as you build that healing place you all can call your own.

From here on out things are going to be uncertain and unpredictable, but by meeting your kids where they live and think, you are making the commitment that you will move forward as a family, even as you are heading into the great unknown.

You'll learn more in Chapter 7 about how transitions can affect grieving kids. When I went off to college in 1996, it had been eight years since my mom died. It was just enough time for everyone around me to adopt the cultural norm that I had "moved on" and was doing great. The truth was, I had barely begun to really grieve.

From the time I got to the University of Virginia, it was the little things that got to me. Every call home that I heard a friend make was like water torture. After spending all this time and all this energy telling myself and others that I was OK, I had to finally admit the sadness and loneliness I felt without my mother.

On the surface, I had been doing pretty well, but what this transition taught me was that doing well on the surface is only part of the battle, and that you can only do so well with grief on any level when you face it alone. Yet I was determined not to fall into the victim trap.

So I plowed on through and excelled, on paper, throughout my four years at college. Then came a whole new transition, to Atlanta and a career in sports marketing. It was exciting, challenging and energizing. I spent a year working on the Chick-fil-A Peach Bowl and then with a client who had a NASCAR sponsorship. I was constantly busy. I was thrilled with the responsibility I was being given. I was on my way to conquering the business world. Or so I thought . . .

Sketching the Future:
A Healing Place Called Kate's Club

There was always that little matter of the tap on the shoulder, and that voice from a couple of years back. I returned to Camp Comfort for a couple of summers, even after moving to Atlanta and starting my career. My father, who still had not had a substantive conversation with me about my grief, would dutifully meet me at the Richmond Airport each time, take me to camp, then take me back to Atlanta. It was his way of being there for me and my grief in one of the only ways he was capable of at that time.

Throughout my years in the business world, my heart and mind wandered back to the experiences at the camp, and I craved the feeling of making a real difference in the lives of kids in such desperate need of things I never had when I was in their shoes. I knew it was time to do something about it. I knew deep down what I really wanted to do was work with these kids and help make a difference in their lives. I just didn't know how I would do it.

One night in an Atlanta restaurant, I sat with my father and shared my desire to combine what I was learning in the business world with this incessant passion to work with these kids. He listened and gave his typically carefully considered thoughts and ideas. Before the night was through, we had ourselves several cocktail napkins' worth of ideas that would become the original blueprint for a place called Kate's Club.

The biggest gift my father gave me that night was confidence and empowerment. It took courage for me to express my wants and desires, but I felt safe sharing them with him. He reacted with excitement and optimism. That was empowering.

It's a lesson I think you can use with your own children, even if you are dealing on a completely different level. The way you respond to their expression and their excitement can empower them to take action. And the willingness and ability to take action is a big part of being a survivor. I happened to be telling my dad about starting a not-for-profit. But it is just as important for you to show this excitement when your kids are talking about an accomplishment at school or a desire to join a team or an organization.

While I looked at the enormity of the task before me, he saw it as an adventure that would help me learn and grow. And most important, he believed in my ability to pull it off. That was all I needed. Well, almost all I needed!

"I Thought You'd Be Old and Wearing Black . . . "

Armed with my father's belief and support, all I had to do was actually make it happen. I quickly began to see that this would not be a simple task. But my feet were wet and I was not about to look back! I will never forget my first meeting with a potential Kate's Club family. I was in an incredibly vulnerable place. I knew I had the passion to build this organization, and the vision for it to become an amazing resource for so many kids and their families. But to make any of that happen I needed the kids. And to get the kids, I needed to make parents believe in me. What, I wondered, could I possibly do to make these parents entrust me with the task of helping their kids through the hardest time of their lives?

There were three girls, ages seven, nine and eleven, who had recently lost their father to cancer. I walked into the coffee shop, dressed professionally and trying to present the image of a trustworthy and responsible person, even though at the ripe old age of twenty-four, I came off looking much more like a friend. I was wearing a pink wrap sweater.

Was this actually going to work?

The littlest girl, before I even made it all the way to the table, looked at her oldest sister and said, "She doesn't look like what I thought she'd look like."

So I asked. "What did you think I'd look like?"

"I thought you'd be old and wearing black."

"Well, I am young, I like to have fun, and I love the color pink. What do you like to do?"

While I engaged the girls in some conversation, I pushed a folder across the table to their mother. It contained my résumé and some personal and professional references. I didn't know what the organization would even look like at this point, so it was not as if I had much to share about it. I just needed the families to be comfortable with me, to accept me and, most important, to trust me. Their mother looked at the folder, looked at me, and said, "Kate, I don't need any of that. I just want you to tell my girls your story."

Well, that was easy. I told them my story. Then I said, "I always felt like I had to walk this grief journey alone. And now that I'm older, I just really want to get to know you and let you know that you don't have to walk your walk alone."

And we began our walk, just as you and I are now beginning ours.

Together.

Kate's Club

This chapter would be incomplete without some background on Kate's Club's history. Not just because it is the impetus for my writing this book, but because its example can show you the simplicity of building a successful healing place for your kids.

When I began this journey, I was just like you. All I had to propel me was my shared experience with these kids and a strong desire to help them. Your shared experience with your kids has the power to forever bond you together or to tear you apart. Yet by choosing to read this book, you are telling me you have chosen the bonding route. Experience and desire are what will carry you along your healing journey, just as they have carried me along mine. They are the first seeds of creating a healing place in your home.

That first meeting with the family of three girls represented the first time I planted these seeds for Kate's Club. It was a raw and unrehearsed meeting of support. The early days of Kate's Club were much the same. This year Kate's Club celebrates its sixth year of serving grieving youth in Atlanta. We have grown from serving six kids to serving hundreds. And with time and resources, our healing place has not only been able to grow in the number of kids we serve, but also in our service capabilities.

Here's how it happened. Our very first club outing was held at a bowling alley and included six kids, six buddies and me.

For the next several months, I would rent a van and travel throughout Atlanta to pick up the kids, whose numbers were steadily growing through word of mouth, and take them to various outings. The whole thing was about making this experience fun for them and providing relief for their families. We took the kids to various venues and events around Atlanta, such as Turner Field, Fernbank Museum and even Whole World Theatre, where the kids got their own private improv comedy workshop.

As more families joined Kate's Club, the minivan was not cutting it anymore. We set up a new system where the families and buddies met at a local bookstore. From there we'd pile into two airport shuttle vans and head out together to the day's destination. Some of the parents also took advantage of this new system and began informally gathering to talk at the bookstore after the kids left. This was an important development and one we will talk about later when we discuss the healing power of peers.

As our organization grew, we realized we had the opportunity to be more than a van to fun locations around the city. We saw the impact we were having already and set our sights higher. We wanted to become a leading resource for grieving children, and we were committed to putting in the time and effort it would take to make that happen. The next big step for us came in August 2005, when we moved into our first permanent space. This "clubhouse," like everything else with Kate's Club, was a true community effort.

Our volunteers came together to get furniture donated and walls painted. The main room received a fabulous makeover from the folks at Turner Broadcasting System.

The whole thing was such a thrill for us, and best of all, it allowed us to spend more time with our kids.

Today we serve hundreds of children, between the ages of five and eighteen, from all over Georgia. We have evolved from a single recreational program to multiple programs that include clinically led support groups and an annual overnight summer camp. Kate's Club has a full-time staff and more than one hundred volunteers who help run its operations, and because of this growth we moved into a newer, bigger Atlanta "clubhouse" in the fall of 2008.

And to think it all started with no money. That's right. Our very first fund-raiser raised just over one thousand dollars, and that was barely enough to get us started. We are very fortunate to have attracted some incredible supporters who have allowed us to grow and help more families than I ever dreamed we could. However, in the beginning, we had only the basic building blocks that you have: love, compassion and hard work.

That's a recipe we all can use.

Kate's Club is only located in Atlanta, but we are not alone. There are remarkable organizations across America who are out there doing the kind of work we do and advocating for kids and families in this situation. I have included a resource list of some of these organizations at the end of the book, and I strongly encourage you to seek out their help whenever possible.

However, what I am doing in this book is more about

creating your own healing place than about referring you to one in the outside world. For it is the work you do within your own four walls that will allow you and your kids to tear down the walls in the outside world that stand between them and the healing and happiness they deserve.

CHAPTER TWO

Communication:
Your Bricks to Building a Healing Place

Anyone dealing with grief is working at a significant cultural disadvantage. We as a society are simply not comfortable with the idea of death and grief. Why is this? I think a big part of it is that we all try hard to live life within our emotional comfort zones. And grief so easily takes us out of our comfort zones. Somehow we've been convinced that it is just not OK to grieve. It makes people around us uncomfortable. They don't know what to say or do. Even worse, it is often seen as a sign of weakness.

So what ends up happening, especially when it comes to kids, is we get caught in a bad cycle. Kids, sensing this discomfort around the topic, end up walking on eggshells for fear of making other people uncomfortable. I know that is what happened to me. Here I had just gone through the worst trauma of my life and I could not feel comfortable raising the topic because others might not be comfortable with it. Then in turn the adults are walking on eggshells around the kids for fear that something they will say or do will send kids into an emotional tailspin.

So in our efforts to protect other people, we mishandle the emotional progression that is really the healthy way to cope with one of life's biggest challenges. Kate's Club is about acknowledging the impact of what has happened to these kids, yet encouraging them to reengage in life and move forward with confidence. And they do! What this confidence allows us to do is break down those walls that people tend to build when they face topics that make them uncomfortable. So how do we get through these walls? That brings us to the crux of this chapter and, in many ways, this whole book. If I had only a single word of advice to offer you it would be this: communicate.

Welcome to the Club

Look at grief this way. You and your child have just become members of a large club that nobody ever wants to join. When I had the privilege of speaking with Rosie O'Donnell on *The View* about her loss (she too lost her mom at an early age), she said, "It's a club that we don't necessarily want to be in, but we all have each other, and we can do it and lift each other up." You are forever bonded by your common loss. There is great strength to be gained from one another. No one else in your lives, not friends, not even many family members, can understand everything you have gone through the way you can understand one another.

In these conversations, one of your most important jobs is to help your children understand that there is absolutely nothing wrong with them because they are grieving. They are not broken. They do not need to be fixed. Most of all, help them understand that even in this club, membership still has its privileges. These privileges include the ability to connect profoundly with others who are sharing their journey. They will learn, with your help, that common ground is healing ground, and that these connections they make will help forge the right path toward a healthy future.

And it all starts with you.

What to Say

Now that we have established the importance of communication, let's talk about how you can make it happen. The most important tip I can give you on this subject is to always be open. This is not an easy thing to do. I remember how hard it was for my family. Your first parental instinct can often be to protect your child, so I totally understand why you might want to avoid conversations that have the potential of exposing your children to more sadness. But I strongly encourage you to push through your hesitation. Some of life's most important conversations can be those that are the hardest to start. Remember the "birds and the bees" talk?

Yet just as with that conversation, you will often find that your child will, ultimately if not immediately, appreciate your reaching across the divide and addressing grief issues directly. If you want children to share honestly with you, do the same with them. Tell them how much you miss their dad or mom. Talk about the things that are giving you a difficult time. By doing that you are welcoming your child into a comfortable sharing place.

Kate's Club dad Norman is raising a teenage daughter on his own, and doing an incredible job of it. He spoke to me recently about some of the things he wished he had done in those early days. "Where I felt I missed the boat, especially early on in the grief process, was not talking to my daughter enough about her mom, not bringing up enough of the good times and asking her questions about how she was feeling."

Now, in their case, after Norman's daughter, Sarah Ann, came to Kate's Club, she opened up more in her conversations with her dad. Being around other kids who were in her shoes and surviving gave her the confidence to understand she was not alone. I can't tell you how often I see this happen at Kate's Club. We'll talk more throughout this book about peer support, but don't underestimate its power to help facilitate healing through communication.

As adults, we can learn from this example. The presence of comfort and a common bond opens a door to discuss grief. Think of this as you approach your own "what to say" moments with your children. And remember that the catalyst here is not necessarily the traditional parent-child relationship. It is the common experience the two of you now share.

Think about how you could engage your child in a conversation about Mom or Dad. I recommend taking out a pad of paper and writing down some starters. One way to broach the subject is by sharing your own emotions. "You know, I really missed Mom the other day when I was working in the garden. It felt strange to be doing it without her. How about you? Have you had times like this? When do you miss her the most?"

In other words, use that shared bond to open up new avenues of shared conversation. And be patient. It might not always work the first time, but as your child's comfort and confidence grows, you can get to some great places. Sarah Ann showed us that.

Mourning the Relationship, Not Just the Person

Another thing the above example shows us is how important it is to talk to our children directly about their particular experiences with their lost loved one.

The common experience of loss can go a long way to fostering communication. However, those common experiences are still limited in this capacity. The reason for this, and the reason that there are no generic cure-alls where grief is concerned, is that grief is relational. When we talk about grief, we are talking about much more than the literal loss of a person. We are talking about mourning the particular day-to-day relationship we had with that person. Understanding this distinction is crucial to being able to help your child, and to your moving through your own grief journey in a healthy way.

At twelve years old, I didn't just miss my mom. I missed going shopping with my mom. I missed coming home to tell my mom every single thing that happened to me that day. I missed her on the sidelines of my basketball games. I missed all those things that were specific to the entity that had been "us." I am sure my brother missed a whole different set of things. Just think of any family you know. Nobody experiences another person exactly in the way you do, and that is never more true than within a family unit. The ties that unite families are woven from intensely personal threads. There is great comfort in the fact that you as a family are united by the love that you shared for this person. However, I urge you to go even further and explore those things that are unique to each person's loss landscape.

Honor those differences when it comes to your child and the relationship she has lost. Again, don't be afraid to engage her in conversation around exactly what it is she misses the most, and at the same time, don't be afraid to share those things that top your own list. Go beyond the words "I know, I miss her/him too." Here is a chance to validate your child's more specific feelings around the loss, to acknowledge that you understand those things that are uniquely his in the grief process. At the same time, sharing those things that are uniquely yours encourages empathy in your child. You are telling her that she is not alone, and in the process you are offering a valuable window into your own heart and soul. This empathy can help immensely in the healing process for everyone involved.

Recently, Norman shared with me that when his daughter Sarah Ann starts talking about her mom, he does everything he can to encourage it. "It's my job as a parent to continue the conversation. I will ask her to go into detail on specific stories. 'Now what did you two do this time or that time?' or 'How did that work?'" I really like the way Norman handles these times. He is really doing two things. He is validating Sarah Ann's need to tell these stories, and he is giving himself a deeper understanding of the personal details of the relationship Sarah Ann lost. This is especially important in his case because he and Sarah Ann's mom had divorced a few years prior to her death.

Norman told me that Sarah Ann's toughest times in those early days tended to come at bedtime. He didn't understand this at first, but he learned through talking with her that this was a particularly special time in Sarah Ann and her mom's relationship. It was a time they would lie in bed and talk, catch up on the day, laugh and just connect. This helped Norman to understand what was going on with Sarah Ann and to talk with her about it and help her move forward.

Remember this with your own child. As much as you think you may know the details and intricacies of the relationship your child has lost, there are probably many things you don't know. Make it a point to engage him about special times he shared with your loved one, even if you know many of them already. You'll be surprised what you might learn in the process.

Acknowledge Your Child's Grief

Just by being open to these conversations, you are taking an important step for and with your child. One of the most helpful and healing things kids can hear is that their loss does not make them "different." Tell them that the only difference can, in fact, be that it makes them stronger. Talk about the unique aspects of your new family. Be open about the fact that change is going to be inevitable. Acknowledge that it is scary, even to you. But be sure to let them know that you are there for them to help weather any storms to come. Make it clear that this is a team effort from here on out. And perhaps most important, tell your kids that, though it might not feel like it now, you will all celebrate great times together again.

One key here is that it is easy for you check in with your own grief. We'll go over this in detail in the next chapter, but it is something you need to consider in your communication with your child as well. If you are having trouble dealing with your own grief, it can keep you from supporting your child in the ways you want and need to do.

Watch for this in yourself. Be aware of those times when you feel "stuck" in your own grief journey and look for ways to break out of them. For example, keeping a journal can be a great way of getting yourself going again. So can opening up to a friend or therapist. You may often find that the things holding you back are things you never even realized were there.

Grief = Love?

I'll say it again. Grief equals love. A major thing that can hold us back in our grief journey is conceding to society's take on grief. We only see the negatives. You may be surprised by this sentence.

Wait. Are you saying there are positives?

The answer is that yes, there are many positives. We all know that sadness is a big part of grief. But we make a big mistake when we make it the only part. Because when you strip grief down to its bare bones, what you really find is love. You and your family could never feel the depths of sorrow you feel without having felt the love from which it comes.

One of the first meetings I had when I started Kate's Club was with a chaplain at a children's hospital in Atlanta. I was always delighted when anyone on the clinical side of things took a meeting with me in those days, as it served as validation for what I was trying to do. What I didn't know was just how inspirational the meeting would be, and how she would forever change and clarify my understanding of grief as a source of great empowerment in our lives.

"I always tell people that they should see grief as a trophy for loving someone so much," she said. "Think about it, you don't truly grieve for people you don't know."

Those two sentences opened up a whole new way of looking at the world for me. She is absolutely right. When we are able to truly grieve, it means we were able to truly love, to put ourselves out there for another person in a deep and meaningful way. It means that we have earned the right not merely to miss that person being here on earth, but in fact to miss the details and emotions surrounding our particular relationship with that person.

Looked at this way, grief becomes something we earned as opposed to a burden with which we are saddled. We need to make it clear that the emotions our kids are feeling are in no way a punishment for the love they felt and the love they received. This realization can become a powerful tool for moving forward with confidence and learning to love and be loved in the future as they deserve to be . . . freely, completely and without reservation.

Use this new outlook on grief to free yourself in your communication with your child. Don't be afraid to claim this "Trophy of Love" and celebrate how you earned it by sharing those memories and reliving those good times.

We have a volunteer at Kate's Club who likes to talk about an ancient Native American saying that goes like this: "The lesson is not completed until passed along." I love this because it gives us the ultimate hammer in the toolbox we are using to build our healing place: seeing grief as something healthy for ourselves, to be shared with our families.

You Can't Control Grief, but You Can Control How You Move Through It

As long as we are on the subject of that toolbox, let's talk a little about how we can, and can't, use the tools inside it. No sense in pulling out a tool if you don't know what you are ultimately going to do with it, is there? Let's start with a basic fact. I don't have a single tool that can make grief go away. If I did, this book would be much shorter and I'd be much richer.

Grief is not a condition, but a life transformation, and just as with other life transformations, you need to look at the big picture of your life and choose your path wisely. I'm always struck by the number of examples in our culture of successful and powerful people who have taken adversity and used it to motivate themselves, including many whose adversity was grief-related.

One person who comes to mind is Katie Couric. Katie went through a very public grieving process when she and her two daughters lost husband/dad Jay Monahan to cancer in 1998. Here she was setting out on her journey while all of America watched. From everything I have read and heard, Katie did a phenomenal job of communicating with her daughters about the loss. At the same time, she has kept her husband's memory alive by working tirelessly to fight colon cancer on his behalf.

There are so many stories of other high-profile people whose loss of a parent at an early age has been a driving force in their careers and lives. I mentioned Rosie O'Donnell earlier. If you watched her over the years on *The View*, you probably heard her talk very openly about the pain of losing her mother at a young age. You can tell by hearing her talk today that she is still greatly impacted by this loss, but chose from a young age to forge her own path and pursue her own dreams. You can find inspirational examples like these nearly everywhere you turn, both in the lives of celebrities and in the lives of people who are part of your own community every day. Their lives are teaching tools for all of us as we work to make the important choices that will set the course for the grief journeys, and the lives, of those we love.

The First Fork in the Road: Victim or Survivor?

One of the most important choices begins to take shape soon after loss occurs. This is the time your child chooses between being a victim and being a survivor.

Here's how that worked in my situation. Our family's response to our loss was a pretty common one. Everyone fended for him- or herself. The whole idea of a family unit as we once knew it dissolved with my mother's death. We tried to get it back using all the usual tools of the trade at that time—individual counseling, group therapy.

We each made our own attempts, in our own ways, to bring our family back together. But there was little hope of that. My father remarried. My brother retreated. I worked hard to assume the role of peacemaker. I adopted a positive persona that I displayed toward everyone in my life. But it wasn't just an external display, it was also an internal battle that I was confronted with for the first time in my life.

Victim or survivor? The choice is the same for kids as it is for adults. Do we wake up each day, even after such tragic loss, and look at the world as a fearful place or as a place of opportunity? Is our glass half-empty or is it half-full?

I knew I wanted to be a happy person. I wanted to be a person who laughed and who had others who enjoyed being around her. In some ways this can be seen as a defense mechanism. But for me, it was the best way I knew to follow my choice and be a survivor.

Unfortunately, this process is not quite as simple as sitting your children down and asking them which of these two roads they want to choose. The good news is that the process is about finding the right tools to ensure that your children ultimately answer the question in the right way. So let's keep building that toolbox!

First let's recognize that these roads are very different. Simply put, the victim road is a short-term fix. These kids are saying that the attention they will receive around being a victim will be enough to sustain them. But what they don't realize is that it will just keep them running in place as opposed to moving ahead. That's where you come in. Your job here is to prove to them that the survivor road is the road to long-term victory.

Here's one great way to do that. Expose them to others who have chosen this path. Kate's Club member Jo is eleven years old, and he lost his father just over two years ago. His dad had suffered a heart attack in late 2001 and had bypass surgery. From that moment on, his health was a constant struggle, with lingering heart and breathing issues landing him in the hospital multiple times and sapping his strength while he fought to hold on for his family. The struggle ended one night in July of 2006 when, after the family had returned from church services and posed for a now poignant family photo, Jo's dad's heart finally gave out.

Jo; his sister, Shamy; and his mom, Selvy, came to Kate's Club soon thereafter. I recently asked Jo, if he had just one piece of advice for others his age who had lost a parent, what would it be? He said it was simple. "I'd just say every day is a new day. I miss my dad a lot. But every day I live life to the fullest."

I was so proud to hear him say that. Those are the words of a survivor. They are the words we hope to hear through our work at Kate's Club, and the kind of words I hope you hear from your own kids during their journeys.

The people you surround your child with don't necessarily have to be on a similar path. It's just about identifying those people who have chosen to live their lives as survivors as opposed to giving in to any kind of challenge life might have put in their paths. By putting those people into your kids' lives, you are offering up an inspiring example that has more power than any words you can share. In my experience, kids are predisposed to choose the survivor path unless adults are standing in the way.

Here's one way you can help clear this path: Before you work to identify the outsiders who will provide these important examples, provide those examples yourself. In the next chapter we are going to deal with the fact that in order to help your child, you must first help yourself. By taking care of your own grief, you are creating a healthy foundation for healing. You are choosing the survivor path, and in the process you are bettering the odds of your child doing so as well.

A Survivor's (Unconventional) Path

We must also acknowledge and respect the role grieving kids can play in forging their own survivor paths, no matter how unconventional they may seem to us as adult observers.

Let's look at the high-profile example of Paris Jackson, the young daughter of Michael Jackson. Few people will forget the moment when she took the microphone at her father's memorial service and expressed how she felt about him and how much she was going to miss him. I was not surprised that there was immediate negative reaction from many who felt that this was putting her in a bad situation or even exploiting her.

I believe these people are missing a crucial point. This was Paris Jackson's moment, her opportunity to gain a measure of control over all that was swirling around her and to honor her father and the relationship she had with him in front of the entire world. During the service, she was gradually moving from the edges of the crowd onstage toward the middle until she finally took center stage. It was a moment she deserved, a chance to express the love she felt for her dad and a moment she will hold on to forever. While most saw this exchange as the point at which Michael Jackson was most humanized, I saw this as an empowering moment at which Paris was humanized, and an inspirational example to the thousands of kids who will stand up and want to speak.

Another example of someone who worked hard to forge her own survivor path, even if it was not one that most people would expect, is Bindi Irwin, the daughter of the late "Croc Hunter," Steve Irwin. Bindi Irwin was only eight when her dad was tragically and very publicly killed in a freak encounter with a stingray off the coast of Australia. Soon after his death, his wife, Terri, made the choice to allow their daughter to continue her father's legacy by hosting her own animal-related TV show. There was a loud outcry from the public that Terri was exploiting her child and the tragedy.

I can't tell you how strongly I disagree with this. To me, this was a mother giving her child an amazing choice to honor her father, and to strengthen her connection to him. Terri Irwin was allowing her daughter to begin her grief journey by learning more about her father and his life. Most important, she was exercising Bindi's desire to feel connected to him and to her family in a context that she was used to already in her life: the zoo. For Bindi, this was her "normal," and it brought her comfort. I applaud Terri for allowing her child to be vocal and to continue her efforts as a young wildlife conservationist, her father's extraordinary legacy.

Terri is a great example of a parent who had a choice, just like you have a choice. And she chose to make her daughter a survivor instead of a victim around her grief. In the process, she illustrated a very important lesson: that grief looks and feels different for everyone.

Right Back to Communication

Communication is the primary tool for building your family's healing place. Without it, you can't even begin to start your healing process. I hope to help you learn to use this tool to communicate not only within your family but in the world outside your home as well, with teachers, counselors, coaches and all the other "players" in your child's world. And eventually, your children will be able to use the communication techniques you teach them to create healing places of their own, with peers, mentors and others who can help.

A healing place is a comfortable place where sharing and communication are open, honest and trusted. Your effort to build one for your kids will be successful if you remember this foundation. Now let's help you move forward with some more specific tips in building this healing place. We're going to start with you.

CHAPTER THREE

Supporting Your Own Grief: The First Step to Helping Your Child

My favorite example to share with parents who are concerned about helping their grieving child is the airliner oxygen mask story. Should an emergency arise, you are told, oxygen masks will fall from above your seat. Then you are told the most important thing of all: if you are traveling with small children or others needing assistance, you are to place the mask on yourself first and *then* assist the person next to you.

In the same way, before you can help your grieving child, you have to help yourself deal with your own loss. I know it goes against your natural parenting instincts, which is to put your child before you, and that is totally understandable. But you can't truly help that child if you don't focus on your own grieving first. You must work to put yourself in a place where you feel strong enough to provide the empowering guidance and examples your child needs.

Children learn to navigate foreign situations by looking around themselves in search of role models. So by taking that time to care for yourself, you are doing two crucial things: you are ensuring that you can be fully there for your child, and you are doing your duty of getting her lifelong grief journey off to a healthy start.

Every Grieving Parent Is Different

Just as every grieving child is different, every grieving parent is too. No one had the exact relationship you had with your loved one. No one else knows the full content of your memory bank. Even your children, who are going through this with you, can't grasp the many dimensions of your loss. Take some time to understand and grasp these yourself. Think about how your loss impacts who you are. The ground you are standing on is shifting under your feet. Don't assume that you can easily move forward as the exact same person you were before.

Andi is a Kate's Club mom who learned this lesson well. Andi and her husband, Paul, were busy preparing for their son's bar mitzvah in the spring of 2003. Paul complained of a headache as he and Andi were working on center-pieces for the big day. She thought little of it and suggested he go to bed, that she could handle the rest of it alone.

Later that night, Paul was rushed to the hospital after suffering seizures and convulsions. Hours later, he was diagnosed with a rare form of pneumococcal meningitis. He quickly fell into a coma. Two days later, he was gone, and Andi was a forty-two-year-old single mother of eleven- and thirteen-year-old boys.

"I read everything there was to read about what I was going through," she told me. "But it was something I was told about a week or two after Paul died that really made an impact. It was to remember to mourn not only for him, but for you, because the person you were died with him. That was so true because I was no longer the same person, or the same parent."

This is such an important point. It's impossible to process all the changes in your new world. Nearly every role of your life has changed. You are taking on a comprehensive parenting role as opposed to being part of a team. You are heading up a household where you once shared responsibilities. In the aftermath of loss everything changes. So don't expect to be the same person you were. Let's look at some ways you can help yourself to ease the transition into a new life.

Acknowledge *Your* Grief

At Kate's Club, we get many calls and emails from adults who have lost a spouse. Generally, they will keep the focus of the conversation entirely on their kids' need for help. They tell the kids' stories, often with great compassion and in great detail, painting a picture of how the loss has impacted the kids' lives. It amazes me how few of them acknowledge that they too have suffered a loss. I respect them for their selflessness and certainly understand their desire to address their kids' need for support, but I also make a mental note that they may be in danger of ignoring their own grief. Remember that you have suffered a great loss too, that your life has been turned upside down. Just because you are an adult and may have the ability and life experience to handle it does not make you immune from the pain of it all.

Your grief is different from your child's grief. Not more, not less, just different. You owe it to yourself and to your family to take whatever time you need to understand the impact of this loss on you. Then you can seek out the tools you need to move forward both as a parent and a person.

There are several significant roadblocks that keep parents from taking care of themselves. One is guilt. When they spend time on their own grief, many parents have told me, they feel like they are neglecting their children. I tell these parents that they need to look at this in another way. Look at it from your child's perspective. What your child needs most is you at your healthiest and strongest. So by taking this time and focusing on yourself, you are actually doing what is best for your child. There is no selfishness involved.

Another potential roadblock is the fear of your own grief. Sometimes when I talk to Kate's Club parents I find that the energy they put into dealing with their children's grief is sometimes a means of distracting them from what they should be feeling themselves. You have to understand that you can never outrun grief. It will find you. And the farther down the road you go before you let yourself feel its impacts, the more disastrous consequences it can have for you and for your family.

Kate's Club dad Norman shares this: "Your children's suffering is right up there with yours. But I just came to the realization that I can't help my daughter with her grief if I can't help myself."

Norman found his greatest help through the support of his peers, specifically those who had been through or were going through grief themselves. But it wasn't easy. "Growing up in a small town, and being a guy, having a father I never saw cry, I had these unreal assumptions of how I was supposed to go through it all. My initial thought was that I just had to drive through it."

A big part of Norman's support system came through his Kate's Club experience. "It's been a big asset for me to identify with parents who have gone through it before. I've benefited greatly from being able to touch base with parents, find out what is going on with their children and share what is going on with mine. We'll ask each other, 'What are the changes you are seeing?' or 'How are you coping?' It just makes you realize you are not alone."

I urge you to find that kind of help wherever you can. It might be through identifying some people in your immediate circle who can provide the most comfort, counsel and support. Or you may find that you're consoled by taking the time to write things down in a journal, as I discussed earlier. Or it might be, as in Norman's case, that you find aid among those who have suffered a similar loss.

Keeping a Connection to Your Loved One

As Norman's example illustrated earlier, Kate's Club parents have formed powerful communities of their own. Sometimes I am fortunate enough to sit in on conversations or group discussions these parents have. And I can tell you that one of the recurring topics is how to keep a connection with a loved one while still moving on with your life.

Grieving parents are all living in a world where their success is measured by their ability to move forward. This goes back to the cultural perceptions of grief we discussed in Chapter 2.

But at the same time it is perfectly understandable and in fact appropriate that these parents often have a strong desire to hold on to the person they have lost. It is a totally healthy and normal desire. In fact, I would be more concerned if you did not want to hang on to this person in some way. We are talking about lives that were intertwined, filled with indelible memories that likely both include and pre-date having children. We'll talk more about how to handle those family memories in a positive way in Chapter 5. For now, I want to keep the focus on you.

By keeping your connection to your loved one, you are honoring both your grief and the person you lost.

Remember that "Trophy of Love" we talked about on page 34? This is about claiming that trophy. After all, you earned it through the love you felt and shared while your loved one was here.

One way you can claim that trophy is by openly talking about your loved one with others. Yes, this may make some people uncomfortable. They might not know how to respond at first. But by opening the door to the conversation, you can facilitate the kind of sharing that is very healing in the long run.

Another avenue to the Trophy of Love is to create your own ways to honor the person you lost. These can include something traditional, like regular visits to a grave site. I know many people who get a lot of comfort from these visits, whether they have a routine of gardening around the site or merely use the time to reflect.

I also know many people who have created their own personal traditions that connect them with their loved one. It could be driving a favorite route you liked to drive together. It could be rewatching a favorite movie you enjoyed together. Or, as hard as this can be, watching family videos that connect you to who your loved one was in your life and family unit. You might want to visit a favorite place you shared, perhaps a beach or park that had an important role in your life. The choices you make here are your own. It's all about finding that place or experience that somehow represents and honors the bond you had.

Table for One

For Kate's Club parent Debrah, comfort comes in the form of a table for one.

Debrah's husband, Melvin, began experiencing some breathing problems in May of 2001. He was treated for what she called a "touch of pneumonia" and released. By Memorial Day he had been hospitalized again. Then, on July 8, Melvin's battle ended and Debrah's new challenges began. She was left with two girls and a boy and, like most people in her situation, very little idea of how she was going to move forward.

Over the years, I've come to be incredibly impressed with the path Debrah has forged for herself and for her kids. She has a developed a great ability to go ahead with her life while honoring the life she had before.

And that is where the "table for one" comes in. She told me once that every year on the anniversary of her wedding to Melvin, she takes herself out to dinner. "It's just my private time," she said. Debrah says she doesn't hide from anyone that she does this—not from her kids (who also know that she arrives at the cemetery each year on Melvin's birthday with a cake or cupcakes), nor from the man to whom she is now married. I find this story incredibly empowering. How great it is that Debrah has decided to honor her love for Melvin and to honor their relationship in this way. In the midst of trying to move forward, and help her kids move forward, she has committed herself to remembering her first husband in her own special way and to keeping that connection alive. I think her journey is easier and she is stronger for it. I urge you to follow her example and find your own place, or place in the heart, to do the same for yourself.

While the goal here is to take care of yourself, there is an added benefit to an exercise like Debrah's. You are also teaching your children an invaluable lesson. You are showing them your continuing commitment to the person you all loved. The message here is that loving completely is worth it, even in the worst possible scenario you have experienced together. You are teaching them how to create and hold on to a legacy forever. Who knows, maybe someday they will create an experience of their own to reach out to the loved one they too lost.

Creating Your Grief Comfort Zone

Everyone going through grief needs a comfort zone to begin the process. Just as parents at Kate's Club find comfort among the group, I encourage you to do the same with the important people in your life. Start with the comfort of close friends and families. Being comfortable with acknowledging your grief with them is going to help you begin to process it and get back on a path of healthy living while grieving.

One thing I have often shared with Kate's Club parents is that whether they realize it or not, their kids are as worried about them as they are about their kids. Your kids are hoping for your happiness every bit as much as you are hoping for theirs. All the caring and energy that was previously spread out between you and your lost loved one has now been transferred completely to you, and then some. That means that in addition to needing you in their lives in the traditional way kids need parents, your children may be keeping a closer eye now on how you are feeling and doing. It's almost a bit of a role reversal at times.

So by going out and seeking those things that bring you happiness, you are effectively setting a great example for your kids. And while inspiring them to move forward themselves, seeing you happy also makes your kids happy,.

"Me Time"

The first step toward acknowledging your own grief and finding your comfort zone is building some Me Time into the course of your busy new life and its challenges. Me Time should be both active and quiet. The goal is to start to process your own grief in a place that is comfortable and safe for you. I know this can be scary. We often feel safer staying busy, because we can keep our emotions from creeping into our heads and assuage a common pitfall for grievers—the fear of being alone.

I understand this fear, and I walked that line myself with my own grief. But it is something you can free yourself from. Start getting your emotions out there. See emoting as progress not regress. If you don't do this, you are risking a volcanic emotional eruption. These emotions will come. And the longer they remain compressed and sealed off, the less control you have over your expression of them.

Go ahead and carve out your own Me Time, whether you have to make special plans or want to take advantage of those that come in your day-to-day life. Perhaps the time comes as part of your bedtime routine, once reserved for conversations with your late spouse. You can continue that conversation if you want to. You can imagine that conversation in your head if you like. Or, again, it can be healing to write in a journal. Or maybe you want to write letters to your loved one. I also recommend sharing your feelings and fears with someone close to you, or with a therapist. If you're not comfortable with this, I recommend finding an online message board and sharing that way.

Are you a spa person? Treat yourself to a massage every now and then, or even a regular regimen. Have you had to cut back on your normal exercise routines since your loss? Get back to them. It is no secret how much a healthy body can impact our emotional states, and that has never been more important for you than it is now. Maybe there is a hobby that you dropped years ago that you've always wanted to revisit, or a brand-new hobby that you've been thinking you'd love to explore.

Spending time volunteering is another way some parents I talk to get outside of the confines of their new lives. This can allow them to get perspective on the world and can make them feel good about reaching out to others in need.

It is not necessarily about how you do it, but just that you make sure to do it somehow. The sooner you understand and embrace the many facets of your new reality, the better chance you have of bringing hope back into your life—sooner than you ever thought you could. A big part of striving toward this place of hope is seeking out those things in your life that make you happy, healthy and whole.

Me Time = Go Time?

Traveling can be an incredible way to get in some Me Time. I'm a big believer in the power of travel to open up your horizons and give you some perspective. I think this is especially powerful in difficult times.

Leaving your kids behind for the first time after a loss is a major step, and can cause a lot of guilt for parents. This was very true for Susan, whose three kids are members of Kate's Club. Susan's husband passed away suddenly from a heart attack while at home helping their young daughter with her homework.

She and I were talking one afternoon when the conversation turned to summer vacation plans. It was the first summer her kids would be spending without their dad, and she had understandable anxiety around that. She had planned a number of fun things for the kids, from summer camps to beach trips. Then she mentioned an annual "girls' getaway" with her friends. It was coming up, and she had gone in past summers, but was going to skip it this particular year. I asked her why, since it sounded like a lot of fun and something she really enjoyed. Susan told me that she just didn't feel right leaving her kids.

But I told her there was *nothing* wrong with taking time out to focus on herself in that situation. The kids would be going to camp and having experiences that would take them away from her. They could certainly handle her going on this trip, especially since she would likely come back refreshed and prepared to be there for them in the ways they needed her to be.

After a little more of this "healthy encouragement," Susan agreed this trip would be a good idea and that it could be an important step in her grieving process. I love Susan's decision. She was making a commitment to do something for herself, something she deserved that would bring her the potential for great enjoyment. And she not only decided to go away, she decided to do so with a group of good friends. I always tell parents that, especially for that first trip, it is great to surround yourself with a person or people very close to you. It helps if your traveling partners understand what you have been going through. You also need to be prepared for the fact that taking yourself out of the realities of your new life may bring forth some emotion. It is always great to have your nearest and dearest around you in these moments.

If taking a trip without your kids seems like too big of a step, then plan a getaway with friends and include the kids. You can still enjoy Me Time while you travel—and remain in the comfort of having your kids there too. This can come with its own challenges, especially when you venture forth as a family for the first time since your loss. We'll talk about that more in Chapter 7, when we talk about transitions.

Your "Me Box"

I've shared some general Me Time suggestions with you, but I also want to help you drill down and create some options that apply specifically to you. Find a pencil, paper and a small box. Think of a few Me Time activities that you would enjoy and write each of them down on a slip of paper. Fold the slips of paper up and drop them in your "Me Box." You don't have to come up with these ideas all at once. Just like everything else on your grief journey, this is an evolving process. Just keep your Me Box handy, and whenever you come up with an idea, fold it up and drop it in.

Then, when you are looking for some Me Time ideas, pull the box out. Reach in and grab a slip. If you can, try to follow through on what is listed. Now, you know and I know that this won't mean you will be able to make all these things happen right away. Yet it's still a great exercise that can open your eyes and your heart to the fact that there are things out there you can do if you want to, and that this Me Time is something you deserve.

Help Is Out There

I am a big believer in the healing power of therapy. At the same time, the importance of making the right connection with the right professional cannot be ignored. Most mental health professionals will honor this need for a connection and will guide you to make sure that you feel comfortable with them. This is an important measure when choosing a therapist. You should *not* settle for anything less than a comfortable connection, a mutual respect and a rapport that allows you to express what you need to.

Use all the resources at your disposal to find the right therapist for you. Talk to your friends, your colleagues . . . anyone who you think might be able to help. The extra work will pay off when you find that perfect match. Remember, though, that this is just a part of your healing process. I always encourage parents to seek out other avenues as well, avenues you can find in the real world every day. There is no better way to find that support than through your peers. It is the cornerstone of Kate's Club, allowing kids to open up where traditional approaches fail. It can and does work the same way for adults.

Some faith institutions and hospices or hospitals can also provide in-person support groups for widows and widowers. So seek help. I know it can be uncomfortable at first, but I'll say it again: *You are not meant to do this alone.* You are not expected to have all the answers and you are not expected to be superhuman and perfectly protect your children while also shielding yourself from all the difficulties grief can bring.

You and your child are moving through an amazing life experience, even if it is one that no one should have to face. It is an experience that offers gifts as well as struggles. Right now life is about getting yourself to the side of the shore that allows you to see and receive these gifts, and to help your child do the same.

The Healing Power of Your Peers

Never underestimate the power of your story. It is something that has the power not only to provide you with a release, but to bring people into your circle who can best support you—whether they are new to your life or were there already. It goes back to Norman's story. His outlet happened to be Kate's Club. And while I wish I could deliver the Kate's Club experience to all of you wherever you are, I can't do that yet. But it doesn't necessarily take a Kate's Club for you to find the support you need from the people around you.

Debrah remembers realizing that what she needed most was a social network that connected her with women who were in her shoes. She just had no idea how to find it. One day after returning to work, she was talking to her boss, who knew someone who had lost her husband several months before. Debrah called her, and as fate would have it, the woman was on the verge of starting a support group for younger widows. The group started with her, Debrah and one other recent widow before they added one more.

"We met initially twice a month for about a year," Debrah said, "and then took it down to once a month." The group still meets once a month, and supplements these meetings with dinners at various points throughout the year. Even after Debrah remarried, she was very clear with everyone in her life that this was something she needed and was going to continue. "I know spouses sometimes don't understand these things, but I made it clear before I got married that this is what I was doing and that these ladies and I are connected forever. We're beyond the point of talking about 'Oh I wish he could come back,' and on to talking about how to deal with blended families and those types of issues."

One of the keys to Kate's Club's success is our ability to use peer interaction to create an even playing field for all our kids. You can find that even playing field in your own circle, in your own community and in your own life. Norman found it in Kate's Club. Debrah found it by reaching out to a person she didn't even know. And another mom found it on her kids' playground.

A woman in her early thirties contacted me after her husband had died suddenly. She was the mother of two and we had a mutual friend who suggested I might be able to help. Her kids were infants and therefore too young for Kate's Club. but she still wanted to connect. It is always inspiring to hear stories like hers, and I hoped that I might be able to provide her with a bit of hope and healing.

She shared her story quickly. Her husband had died just weeks before the birth of their second child. At the time she called me, she had been living life as a single mom for a year. She said she felt fortunate to have a strong family support system both from her husband's family and from her own. Yet she was struggling with something. She felt that every time she took her kids to the playground she found herself trying to fit in with the other mothers, yet she could not help but feel some bitterness toward them. She found herself wanting to express and explain her grief to women who had absolutely no idea what she was going through.

We talked about the possibility of her starting a playground group for young widows, and she ended up doing just that. The results were helpful and healing. She said she was amazed and comforted to know that there were others in her community who shared similar struggles. The group became a support group in the very purest of forms—a collection of people bound together by a mutual understanding that can only come from a true experiential connection.

The common thread weaving together all three of these people I've mentioned is their stories. By feeling confident enough to share their stories and to hear the stories of others, they created communities. And those communities became important healing places for all of them.

The Faith Connection

Many families find great strength from their faith and from their faith-based communities. Faith and spirituality can play a huge role in binding people together and in shaping an individual's interpretation of grief. If your family had a strong spiritual life before, there is no reason to stop after your loss. I am not going to talk too much about faith in this book, because as I have seen in Kate's Club, this is a very personal choice and plays a diverse role in the process of handling grief and death for different people.

Selvy, Jo and Shamy (whom we met in Chapter 2) are a great example of a family whose faith provided and continues to provide great strength. They share a strong Christian faith and are deeply involved and connected with their church in Atlanta. "We've always been a religious family," said nineteen-year-old Shamy. "Dad always had a heart for church and made sure we always had faith in us."

That faith was put to the ultimate test when Dad Josiah passed away. His wife, Selvy, explained that after a heart attack and subsequent bypass surgery, Josiah's health was never the same. Yet he battled on for as long as he could, until that fateful night that he collapsed. Because the family had moved to the United States without their extended family, Josiah's death presented a difficult obstacle in finding people to reach out to. "We did not have any family in this country," Selvy said. "That was very hard. So, in a way, our church became our family. I still talk often with ladies in our church and with our pastor's wife and gain great support from them."

Here is an example of a surviving parent using her faith as a support base not just in prayer or meditation, but in reaching out to her faith community for grief support. I highly recommend that if you are involved in a faith community, you take advantage of the support it can offer you—not only in the immediate days, weeks and months after your loss, but for as long as it gives you comfort.

Your Support List

The examples I have shared represent people who have found support in a variety of ways. They were fortunate to find others they could reach out to, but at the same time, they worked hard to create the networks that would sustain them on their journeys. If you're feeling overwhelmed and are not sure where to turn for support, here's an exercise that can help you sort out your needs and figure out who can help you.

Since there are few things more overwhelming than the challenges that face grieving parents and families, a simple solution is to make a list. Start by taking a step back from your life for just a moment. Think about the changes your loss has brought to your life and your kids' lives. The challenges facing you have literally multiplied overnight.

Acknowledge this by listing the challenges you face or will face, and lend yourself some understanding about them. Here's just a start of a list that may resemble your own: single income, raising a child that is the opposite gender, single disciplinarian, single emotional caregiver. It's a list that can become lengthy, but only you can determine its length, due to the variables in your situation.

This list may be an overwhelming exercise at first, but it is a practical one that provides you with an important window into your new role as a person and as a parent. The more you are able to acknowledge and accept these changes and challenges, the more you will be on your way to tackling them. And it is my hope that by laying all this out in front of yourself, you might see how tough things are and make life a little easier on yourself.

The second step of this list-writing process is looking at each item and writing down where you think you will most need help. Once you do this, it is on to step three, which may be done a little later. In step three, you write down what friends, family members or contacts might be able to help you with each of these challenges. Understand that there are many people in your life who want to help you, and that you may have no idea how to ask them to. It comes down to this: it's up to you. Do you sit there and allow these important resources to stand on the sidelines, or do you bring them into the game? I am here to tell you that you must bring them into the game, and quickly!

Take a good look at that list of people and prioritize whom you would like to contact and how you would like to do it. You can reach out by making some phone calls or sending some emails. When you do, be honest about why you are contacting the person. It is never easy to ask for help, but in this case it is absolutely necessary.

Maybe you're a father raising a teenage girl and you are looking at a whole range of issues on the horizon. Is there a female figure who has a good relationship with your daughter and who you think would be helpful? Ask her to take your daughter out shopping or out for lunch or to an event. It's not about asking people to have a certain conversation or to tackle a sensitive issue. It's about asking them to make themselves available as resources. You're likely to find that more people want to help than know how to help. Your reaching out to them gets the process going for everyone.

This is not meant to put pressure on you at a time when you have more than enough to handle. I'm not suggesting you contact all these people at once. My hope is that just by having that list together you can gain a measure of strength from knowing there are people out there for you.

Go back to your list every once in a while. You'll find it will change as your kids grow and as your mutual journey continues. This list can help you think of and see where your comfort zone lies in asking for help, and begin to empower you to do so.

Creating the Emotional Comfort Zone
for Your Kids

Much of this chapter has focused on creating that emotional comfort zone for you. Now I want to finish up with some ways you can create an emotional comfort zone for your kids. Many parents I talk to tell me how hard it is for them to "stay strong" for their children in the aftermath of a loss. Kids are going to look to parents for safety and stability. And to some extent, they are going to look to parents as a gauge of how they should be handling the massive tremors that have hit their families and their lives. Kids will look for you to still be Mom or Dad—they will be searching for routine and a sense of normalcy. So when it comes to the basics, like having lunches packed, sticking to the usual routines you had with your kids before will help your kids understand that both they and you are going to be OK.

There is something else they are looking for, however, that is going to be more important in the long run. Your kids are going to be looking for validation of their own reactions and emotions. By seeing you emote, they can begin to see and accept their own emotions and express them in a healthy way. I urge you to continually invite your child into your grieving process. Talk to him on your good days and bad days. Talk to her about those memories you are holding on to and why. Talk about your child's parent, who he or she was, funny stories and sad stories. This can take place in a very informal fashion, at the dinner table, on a walk. You'll find there is great comfort and healing in setting the example that you and your child are on a shared journey.

I recently asked Selvy, Jo and Shamy what gave them the most strength on their journey. They said it was the fact that they were never afraid to share their thoughts and feelings about Josiah and about their loss. "All I can say," Selvy said, "is that we needed to talk about what we did with him and appreciate when he was here, what we accomplished together. And we needed to talk about how thankful we are for all that happened."

"We are very open with each other," nineteen-year-old daughter Shamy said, "and we've always been that way, since I was little. There were never a lot of secrets to keep within our family, and that was true before my dad died and after."

The more you let your kids see you dealing with your grief in healthy and balanced ways, the better chance you are giving them to grieve healthily. Never forget that no matter what help you seek for your child outside of the home, the experience of grief that he has within your four walls is going to be most important. Parents sometimes look to therapists or organizations like Kate's Club as a magic healer, not taking into account the fact that these kids are only with outside organizations for a few hours, or a few days, at a time. You yourself have the power to create the environment that will determine how comfortable your kids are about expressing their grief emotions.

At Kate's Club, we regularly see that the kids who are encouraged to grieve and emote at home and in the presence of their families tend to be the leaders. By giving your kids a head start, you are greatly increasing their chances of finding comfort and healing through other channels, be they relationships or organizations such as ours.

One of these leaders at Kate's Club is a young girl who lost her dad. She has always been an example to me of a healthy grieving child. She is often the first child to welcome a new member, and the other kids tend to gravitate toward her during support activities. She once sent me a note that read, "Since my father passed away, my family's motto has been 'faith, family, and friends.' Through Kate's Club, I have found faith in the future, hope for my family, and friends who I can talk and relate to."

I loved this note because it gave such mature insight into the three most important factors to any child, especially a grieving child: future, family and friends. Your job is to do everything you can to make sure your child finds that hope in you that lets her know these three things are not only real, but still attainable. In the chapters that follow we will give you some tools to get you started on building this comfort zone and, ultimately, a sustained environment within your home that is healing and uniting for your kids.

CHAPTER FOUR

Your Child's Voice:
A Key to Healthy Grieving

As Chapters 1 and 2 have emphasized, communication is our number one tool for building a healing place for you and your children. Grief isn't visible, so without communication and expression, healing can't even begin. Like many who have studied and tackled the subject of grief, I hesitate to offer step-by-step advice for the best ways to handle it, since the process will be so different for each person. However, I can say, from both my own experiences and those of the families I have worked with, that there is one key that is an absolute must when coping with grief: you must find your voice.

This goes for you and for your children. In a world where it feels like everything has been taken away from them, kids are desperate to find a voice that will let them share their thoughts and feelings and provide a platform for the swirl of emotions defining their new life.

Finding this voice can be a tricky business. It is not as simple as finding a voice in the literal sense. That would be an unfair advantage for the Mariah Careys of the world. Just sing out your troubles and you'll feel better. And come to think of it, we do often hear singers talk about how therapeutic their gift can be in this way. If only we all had access to that kind of outlet. But the truth is we *do* all have access to our own outlets, and to our own voices. I've seen them discovered and utilized in countless ways—some predictable and some completely out of left field.

Think of a grieving child's voice as a vehicle, as a means through which he can express thoughts and feelings that help him move forward. So how do we find these voices? I wish I could tell you there was a secret formula. Your child's voice won't necessarily be discovered in an AHA! Moment, like mine was that night in the Virginia camp. It felt to me like my voice magically appeared that night in a single, powerful moment of discovery. The truth is that I know it had been developing for years. It was just developing in an unusual way.

Ultimately your child's voice will help her communicate her thoughts through her words and actions. No one can ignore or silence his or her own emotions. But a truly healthy grieving person listens, processes these emotions and expresses them through healthy, positive action.

She Shoots . . . She Scores!

Basketball was my sanctuary, the place where I found safety and comfort. It was particularly appropriate for me because the sport kept me connected to my mom in very literal and profound ways. She was my coach, she was my cheerleader and she was definitely my biggest fan, from the first time I picked up a ball to the last time she coached me on the sidelines, even while restrained by her oxygen tank.

Basketball was a connection I had to my mom. I never remember consciously deciding to stick with it after she died, but my desire to excel in the sport definitely jumped a notch as I entered into my teen years without her. Looking back, I realize that basketball provided me with a place to express my emotions and exercise my energy, good and bad. This kind of activity can provide a recognizable voice for any child. Kids attach to activities and hobbies. Some strive for accomplishment, and all search for a sense of purpose within them.

As my basketball connections deepened, my passion for the game became about far more than my mom. The game had given me a safe and healthy place to express some of my feelings surrounding my loss without my (or anyone else) even knowing it. I could be joyful. I could get angry. I could even cry and not feel self-conscious about it. I was learning that crying in the locker room, among my teammates, was totally acceptable—far more so, in fact, than crying about the loss of my mother. I felt validated expressing emotions surrounding winning and losing, and the people around me were comfortable with it because that is what kids do.

Grieving Kids and Emotions: Between a Rock and a Hard Place

Emoting in our culture is often handled in an extremely hypocritical manner. People are likely to extend more compassion and comfort to someone who is upset over losing a ball game than someone who is upset over losing a parent. As I've said, emotions surrounding grief are too often seen as a sign of instability. This is one of the biggest injustices we teach our kids, and the irony of this stigma blows my mind. It is a challenge to these kids' maturity that they are thrown into the deep end of the adult-size pool of emotions without any warning or preparation. Yet we hesitate to give them the respect they deserve for this. Instead we use words and phrases like "resilient" and "bouncing back" as if to reward them for not letting an event like this impact their lives.

Let's be real. Grief impacts every one of us, at any age. We don't suddenly develop emotions at some point during our lives; we are born with them. Our ability to express these emotions in healthy ways depends on our self-confidence and our understanding of who we really are. This puts grieving kids at a huge disadvantage. They are just trying to figure all that out when they're hit with this blow.

So when we call a grieving child "resilient," we are

taking away the journey of his healing process. Because the child is not as able as we are to emote, we assume that she must be somehow magically able to pick herself up and move forward. We are assuming that children don't completely understand the impact of what has happened.

I much prefer the word "courageous" to "resilient," because kids *do* understand the impact of loss on their lives. And they are actively and bravely trying to adapt to those changes and move forward. It just takes them longer to put that action behind their thoughts. It takes them longer to find their voice.

When it comes to emotions and expressions, kids are stuck between a rock and a hard place. If they express emotions, they fear they will isolate themselves, that they will be labeled as emotionally weak. If they are not expressive, we all worry. All the while, they battle the ultimate challenge: trying to live in a kid's world of innocence and happiness *and* in an adult world of healthy expression of anger and sadness.

I've been in their shoes. I can see it in their eyes, and I understand the enormity of the challenges they face. You as a parent must understand it too.

More Than Words

That is the first step to helping your child find his voice. You have to take into account the line he is straddling between child and adult. The approach many adults tend to take is to look for a traditional voice from grieving kids. We search for words pulled straight out of Webster's dictionary. But the spectrum of emotions is much larger than the entire list of adjectives in the dictionary. Therefore we have to help these kids find alternative ways to express their grief. This can be very difficult for a child who is also engaged in the process of finding her new place in the world, a place where she can experience the comfort and safety that have been taken away from her by her loss.

The kids at Kate's Club have a great benefit handed to them. They have a place where they are greeted with comfort each time they open the door. I want to empower you to create such a place for your child in your home.

In my perfect world, all kids would have access to a Kate's Club type of experience. But if this direct outlet doesn't exist, or if it doesn't seem to be working for your child, all hope is not lost. Remember, I didn't have a Kate's Club, but I still had a safe place to develop my voice. Just keep your eyes, ears and heart open and be aware that creating this safe haven for your child may be a matter more of seeking the right roads than of seeking the right words. The most common place to look is where your child expressed himself before Mom or Dad died. I played basketball before my mom passed. It just took on a deeper level of significance in my life after she died. Your child has already most likely found an outlet to discover her voice, be it through sports, dance, arts, theater, music, etc. As her parent, be aware of this and encourage this activity to continue after

Mom or Dad has died. We'll talk a little bit about routine in your child's life in Chapter 7.

Another approach, if your child doesn't seem to have an outlet or activity of this kind in his life, is to give him a gift that he can invest in and learn from. My first suggestion would be a camera. You can also offer to sign your child up for a new class. A dance class, for example, or an art class, can have the double benefit of immersing her in a new activity while allowing her to interact with a new group of kids at the same time.

There are countless ideas here. Many find that a new pet can be a great healing outlet for a grieving child. This combination of bond-forming and responsibility can do a lot to help a child find a balance of joy against the sadness that is so much of a part of his changed life. Plus, the relationship with a pet can provide a new place for him to put his energy and affection. In the end, you'll have to decide what is the best fit for your home.

The discovery of a child's voice is inevitably a bit of a process. And that's OK. Just be patient. At Kate's Club, we provide our kids with a palette of activities that vary from music to art to animals, activities that allow them to discover what is most comfortable and fitting to them as individuals. These are the same strategies you can employ in your own home and life.

Introduce your kids to a variety of activities and see how they best respond. It may be as private as writing poetry or as public as joining a theater group. Ultimately it's up to them. Your primary role here is to guide them and give them options if they need them. This is also a great opportunity to unite you as a family. I find it is especially helpful with your older kids. By sharing activities with them, you can turn the journey of finding their voice into a great connecting exercise that can improve and keep open that all-important communication channel as they continue to grow and mature.

Is Traditional Therapy the Answer?

Now, your child might be one of those kids who can easily express their grief through words and direct narration. Or she may be one whose voice emerges on a page or a stage. Kids develop at their own emotional pace. If they are not comfortable with or even capable of verbalizing their grief, our efforts to force it out of them may only do more damage.

Often, the first place parents turn is to psychotherapy. I've said it before and I'll say it again: I believe this has great healing power if done in the right way, at the right time and with the right professionals. The right therapist will provide beneficial insight and a professional assessment of your child's well-being. It's all about making the right connection, finding that right person who clicks with your child in a way that creates a safety zone where your child can feel good about sharing thoughts and feelings he may have never shared before. Your child may be resistant to this vehicle of grief support, especially if it is offered one-on-one. This may require a little parental enforcement the first few times, but if therapy doesn't seem to be taking with your child, know and respect that the time just may not be right. In a child's mind, being singled out is a bad thing, something that suggests she is doing something wrong or is not meeting expectations placed upon her. For this reason, group therapy may be more easily accepted by your child.

My experience with family therapy following my mom's death was classic: the moping kids in the car, the silent frustration boiling in us all as we drove to each appointment. But the fact remains that we tried. And especially when you are forced to navigate your way through such uncharted territory, sometimes trying is all you can do.

My dad, my brother and I would inevitably take the three seats farthest apart from one another. The therapist would ask questions; my father would answer. The doctor would try to steer the conversation to my brother and me, but we would just pick at each other.

One time I remember the therapist asking me how I was doing. I was so fed up with my brother and father (or at least I thought it was about them) that I just went off about their complete lack of help on the domestic front. The house was a mess, they never did dishes, and worst of all, there was the unbearable sight of ants taking over our sink. Here I was expressing a complete unhappiness and anger. It was probably the first time my father and brother had witnessed such intense emotion from me after our loss. And I was using ants as the cause of my distress. I share this as just one example of how your child could become expressive without directly touching on the death or his grief.

The funny thing is ants remain my kryptonite to this day. This coming from a girl who, when younger, could routinely pick up spiders or usher big bugs out the door without flinching!

The three of us have actually joked about this over the years, but in that session, for me, it was very, very real. I was unable to associate my anger with mature words or feelings around grief. I just knew I hated those freaking little ants. It was my voice even though my words weren't directing a conversation around grief. I was still learning to find the comfort and safety needed for me to directly communicate about my loss, all within the vocabulary I had in my young mind.

I didn't feel completely safe in that room with a therapist, and therefore I didn't express myself directly. Your child's voice will evolve in the place and in the manner she feels safe and comfortable. It's a huge measure of success for us at Kate's Club, and it should be for your home as well. Don't get frustrated if it takes some time. Work with your child to bring it out. It can come when you least expect it. And when it does, it is important that you acknowledge the expression and try to follow it up with some conversation that makes your child feel even safer and more willing to share. Again, I do believe that therapy *can* be helpful for you and for your kids. It just has to be offered in the right setting by the right person, and it must come with the right expectations on your part. What I am suggesting is that you treat therapy as *an* answer, not *the* answer, and supplement it with other experiences, including peer and family support as well as appropriate programs and organizations in your area.

Kids Helping Kids Find Voices

In the years I have been working not just through my own grief, but in support of others' grief, I have noticed a fundamental difference between adults and kids when it comes to grief. Adults are paralyzed. Kids are motorized.

It is a primary observation that allows the work at Kate's Club to provide such a great opportunity for a grief-stricken child to develop into a healthy, happy child. It is why it is such a miracle for me at Kate's Club to watch the power of kids being kids, with kids. I still marvel at their ability to access and discuss their feelings about grief and loss in the most natural and wonderful ways.

In the beginning, those shuttle rides around Atlanta were amazing times where voices were developed and matured. With a single question asked or memory shared, the conversation would erupt. Today that same simple exercise happens right inside the doors of the clubhouse. Who died, how they died, what bothers kids most about having friends react differently to them after the event, how hard it was to go back to school and more. As someone who has been in their shoes but not afforded the same comfort zone, it is amazing for me to see how comfortable they are with one another and how open they are to sharing their stories.

Kids are often more comfortable sharing their feelings with peers than they are sharing them with you. And it's not necessarily because they don't feel safe with you. Many times, I think it is because they are afraid of upsetting you.

I will share my own experience with this. The last thing I wanted to do was upset the emotional apple cart in our house and hurt my dad. So I did what most kids do. I learned every possible way to keep this from happening— even if it came at the expense of my own happiness and emotional development.

Understand that the last thing any grieving child wants to do is upset his surviving parent. Kids learn every possible way to avoid this happening, often at the great expense of their own well-being. No one walks around the house with a grief schedule that tells a child when it is OK to be sad about Dad dying or angry about Mom dying. So if that child is going through a particularly sad time, she is not about to risk sharing it with a mother, father or sibling. So what does she do? She wraps it all up in a nice, tight and sometimes impenetrable ball of silence.

The difference is that adults have to *ask* a kid to share about his grief. Kids only have to *show* one another that it is a safe thing to do. They show this by sharing first and then by graciously accepting others for their own stories and their own grief. Your child's voice may first be discovered outside of your home, and with that confidence she can bring it back to you. When she does, be ready. Be prepared to listen and encourage your child to be confident and comfortable with using it.

I remember overhearing an exchange between a teenage boy and girl one afternoon at Kate's Club. He asked who she had lost in her life. In any other setting this would be an odd, awkward exchange. At Kate's Club it is understood. She explained that she had lost her younger brother. The boy responded, "I know how you feel. I lost my sister."

It was as simple as that. Two people reaching across all the societal boundaries placed on grief and loss and connecting around a shared reality. I remember in those first Kate's Club outings that many of those early parents would pick up their kids in the bookstore parking lot and approach me. "Did they," they would ask, "talk about *it*?"

When I said that they had, I would often get a look of surprise or, in many cases, relief. And sometimes both. The parents just could not imagine that their kids, who had been keeping these emotions so deep inside, were now sharing them with near strangers. Hearing that their chidren had shared in this way was often all these parents needed to know that Kate's Club was a good and safe place for their kids.

What I have experienced is that if these kids first find

that comfort among other kids, they will bring that comfort back into their own homes. I know it may sound a little backward. We've all heard how blood is thicker than water, right? But it is because of the very protectiveness that comes with these family ties that it sometimes becomes easier for children to learn to process grief and emotions among their peers. I am proud that Kate's Club has been recognized as a place that helps kids help one another, but we are hardly alone. There are organizations all over the country that can provide this benefit, and I have included a list in the back of this book to help you locate one.

Patience, Patience, Patience

So as you start exploring how you can support your child, remember the kids' world they left and the adult world they've entered. We tend to expect children to have the same emotional vocabularies we do. That is a mistake. Just think about all we are already asking of these kids and be patient with their voice-finding process! If they are participating in activities, be it sports, crafts, dance or other outlets, then they are expressing themselves. That is a healthy start.

I'll reiterate a key point here: be patient. Your grief and the emotions that result from it may come to the surface a little bit faster and in a little bit more of a direct way than your child's.

Norman shared that in the days and weeks following his ex-wife's death, he did not get the response he expected from his daughter. "To be honest with you, I was concerned about her lack of grief," he said. "It was really strange to me that I was divorced from her mother and I felt like I was having a more difficult time with grief than she was. I had some admiration for her, but as time went on and I was not seeing emotional outbursts or even crying, I was really concerned."

About a month after Stacey's passing, Norman found some information about Kate's Club on the Internet and reached out to us. Not long after that, he said, he began to see the signs he had been looking for, and in a big way. "As soon as it came, boy did it come!"

This is a pretty common scenario I've seen with our Kate's Club kids. They may arrive somewhat blocked in their grief and emotions. Then by sharing their thoughts and feelings and experiencing that common ground they have never experienced before with other kids, they find safety in sharing. Sometimes it's like a floodgate is opened and the pent-up emotions come rushing through. In Norman's case, his daughter used the voices of others to help find hers. It was such an important step for her and for her dad.

Just as Norman said and as we discussed in Chapter 3, remember that if you are addressing your own emotions and grief in a healthy and open way, there is a good chance that your child will follow your lead. If your grief is not expressed in a healthy way, then it may keep your child from seeing the benefit in discovering his own voice.

Try to keep that in mind as you move along your mutual journeys.

If your expectation is for your child to openly and honestly share her grief in front of you, it is time to readjust your sights. That may come in time, especially if you show her that you are comfortable sharing yours in front of her.

Norman's daughter Sarah Ann used common experiences and stories to find her verbal voice. This may not happen with your child, and if it does, it may not happen as quickly. That's OK. I didn't find my verbal voice until I was twenty years old. That doesn't mean, however, that I didn't find another voice when I was younger.

As I said, basketball was more than a game to me. Basketball was a way to express myself, a way to experience the world and make some sense of the swirl of emotions I was feeling. It was, in a word, my voice.

The key is in knowing how to recognize your child's nonverbal voice and to encourage its development. I am forever grateful that my dad got this when it came to my basketball. Each summer he allowed me to go to new camps and meet new people, in the process giving me more confidence than anything else could have given me at the time. But it went beyond that. He helped make basketball not only my voice, but the voice that connected the two of us.

Our relationship had clearly suffered since my mom died. All of life's rules had changed, and neither one of us knew where we fit, including within our family and for each other. Yet the confidence I was gaining on the basketball court then transitioned into a voice I could share with my father. My father played an active role in supporting this activity of mine, and that support sent me a message of love and comfort. It was a message that bonded us and ultimately allowed us to connect in more direct ways around our grief and the passing of my mother.

Furthermore, it was empowering for me to hear my dad's belief in me. It was more than enough to keep me feeling hopeful and strong.

How to Find the Right Outlets

So for my dad, it was pretty easy. Basketball was clearly my thing. But what if you are not seeing that obvious voice emerging in your child? The first thing I would urge you to do is to step back. We have a lot of expectations for what our kids will do or like. It might be a sport or an instrument you played, or some other dream you have had for their futures. As I mentioned earlier, finding your child's voice can sometimes be a bit of trial and error. At Kate's Club, the kids join us as strangers, so we really don't know what their likes and dislikes are. Take what you knew about your child before the death of Mom or Dad and use that as your compass. But remain open-minded and flexible. The changes in your child's life could point him toward new interests and new passions. Be aware of this journey and follow along.

Here's a good example of what paying attention and following along can do for you and your child. I'll never forget the story of Andrew, a young boy who came to Kate's Club at the age of eight.

He joined with his two brothers, one older and one younger, after their father had died. In working with this young boy for several months, I got little action from him on his visits to Kate's Club. He would come in and mope, stare at the others with anger and barely speak for the entire program. He was clearly hurt. He clearly had a lot of anger. And he was clearly stuck. No matter the activity we offered him, he never responded. It would have been easy for us to throw up our hands and give up on him. Instead, we remained patient, creative and supportive. We continued to believe that one day, something would click and ignite an interest.

One of my friends in college was a star football player who ended up being in the NFL. We had known each other throughout school, but our relationship was strengthened even further by a common understanding and a shared experience that forged his bond with Kate's Club. He had lost his older brother when he was only eleven years old.

So one day, thanks to his efforts, a bunch of Kate's Club kids got the privilege of visiting his team's training camp. The kids were completely beside themselves as they stared in amazement at their heroes right there in the flesh. The true amazement really appeared on their faces when some of the star players came over to visit with them. One of the biggest stars of all even took the time to share his own personal story of losing his mother.

At this point in Andrew's involvement with Kate's Club, we had not been successful in getting any response out of him, grief- or non-grief-related. He seemed to be absent, although he physically attended our programs. I always sensed with him that within just a few years, as he grew into adolescence, he would be facing a minefield of bad choices and too many opportunities to make any one of them.

Yet that day at the NFL practice, we received that first response from him. There was a positive reaction that told us he was connecting to the experience of watching these players on a level deeper than your basic sports hero worship. His head was up. He stood close to the field and close to the players. He was engaged—a good sign for any child searching for his or her voice. So later, back at the clubhouse, I mentioned my hunch to one of our Kate's Club buddies, who play such a vital role in our organization by building real-life bridges to our kids. I suggested that he might want to take Andrew outside and play some catch on the lawn.

Bingo. The spark had indeed been lit, and now it was just about providing the right encouragement. For the months following, Andrew would be one of the first to ask to play outside. He played soccer. He played Ultimate Frisbee. He even won the apple bobbing contest that year at the Halloween party. He found his competitive spirit. He found a voice. My hope for Andrew is that he will continue to use this outlet to empower his life and channel his grief in a healthy way. Athletics is just one avenue. It could be music, or drama, or drawing, painting, sculpture, technology . . . The list goes on and on. It can happen over time, as you support your child's instincts or first signs. She might show interest in a television show on a subject you didn't know she cared about. He might just casually mention a new interest in a conversation, and then do it again. Your job is to hear it, to encourage it and to support the interest moving forward.

And it may not reveal itself in your presence. Don't let this frustrate you. In Norman's experience it took an outside source, such as Kate's Club, to get the fire lit in his daughter. The key was that once she felt safe to express her grief in that outside setting, he recognized it, encouraged it and appropriately transferred this safety back to their home.

Dance Dance Evolution

One of my all-time favorite Kate's Club stories is about a young boy who came to us because he had recently lost his mother. Not only did he lose his mom, but because his parents were divorced, he was now living with a new family.

Scott was one of those kids who had a great spirit, but an oversize hunger for attention that often made him a handful for our staff and buddies. The constant grabs for attention were the way he had been conditioned to express his voice, especially in his new life. It was the only way he knew to get what he wanted, and it was not healthy. This is especially difficult in our day-to-day activities. This behavior was incredibly detrimental to what we were trying to accomplish.

We recognized that what Scott was really looking for was validation and attention. We knew he was battling a sense of abandonment and an erosion of self-worth. It was especially painful for him because in his case, his perceived lifelong support system and companion had chosen to take her own life.

So what was the tipping point for Scott? Believe it or not, it came during the dance that took place at our annual three-day summer camp. No, this was not the night he discovered that he was the next Michael Jackson. In fact, it was particularly noteworthy because the opposite was true. Scott was not much of a dancer at all. But there he was, in the middle of a throng of his friends and peers, dancing his heart out and being wildly cheered for doing so. Who cared how good he was? He was being accepted and acknowledged, things he had been searching for ever since he lost his mom.

We closed the camp session that year with a balloon release. Each child got to write a message to the loved one he or she had lost, tag it to a balloon and then the entire group headed out to an open field for a ceremonial release. Scott proudly showed his note to some of the Buddies.

It read:

Dear Mom,

> *At camp this year, I danced like I never danced before.*
> *I miss you.*

> *I love you—*

There it was . . . a voice . . . a clear expression of pride and, most important, a clear expression of hope.

Looking for the Voice, or the Absence of It

I wish I could give you a surefire secret for finding your child's voice. But the truth is, just as every grieving child is different, so is the process of finding his or her voice. More than anything, it is about being present, about being vigilant. It is about staying close to an understanding of who your child was, is and is becoming in the aftermath of loss.

Here's another way to look at it. Rather than look for the voice itself, you might want to look for the absence of it. When a child starts to steer in the direction of bad activities and patterns, it is as sure a sign as any that that child is searching for a voice and, for whatever reason, not finding one. So while you may also still be in the dark about what form that voice might ultimately take, your first step will be to look for signs that the search is on.

One of the most powerful statements a Kate's Club teen has ever shared was "Without Kate's Club, I'd probably be in jail . . . or sitting home doing nothing."

For a kid like this one, just being able to say this was huge. A voice is a sign of moving forward, and distractions and bad choices are roadblocks to moving forward. These voices must become positive outlets and be received with encouragement and love. A voice can be the thing that makes that child visible again.

Not everyone can be a singer, or an athlete, or a dancer. But everyone wants to be someone. Who is that someone for your child? Maybe you can find it in something he showed you before he lost his mom or dad. In that case, watch for signs that your child wants to continue in that direction. Maybe she will want to leave those earlier interests behind, and that is fine too.

Your job is to watch and listen like your child's happiness depends on it, because it truly can.

CHAPTER FIVE

Memories:
Embrace Them, Don't Erase Them

Now that we've covered the importance of your child's voice, which is the vehicle of expression, we are going to spend this chapter focusing on the *fuel* of that expression: memories. In building your healing place, memories are magic, in that they are both tools for you to support your child's grief and fuel for you to continue your own quest for healthy healing.

Memories are the building blocks of all history, and that is especially true when it comes to families. With that in mind, I want you to consider your role as the memory keeper for your children. Depending on her age, a child's memory of a lost loved one may rest almost entirely with you. You have a unique ability, and responsibility, to pass these memories along and to help complete the picture of the person lost.

Even more important, you can provide a picture of what the "whole" family looked and felt like. Family dynamics are difficult and complex whether loss is involved or not. Yet there is one common thread. Every family is forever linked by those people, places, events and things they share.

Memories are the ultimate adhesive that can bring you together when emotions, events and life itself all seem intent on pulling you apart. This chapter will help you use your memories to build these important bridges to support your child throughout the grief journey.

Oscar Wilde once wrote, "Memory is the diary that we all carry about with us." In technical, psychological terms, memory is described as an organism's ability to store, retain and retrieve information. Yet perhaps we can never truly appreciate the real definition of memory until we lose someone important to us.

Here's a confession. In the hours and days after my mom died, I constantly found myself in her bedroom, burying my face as deep as it could go in her pillow, where I could still literally breathe her in. It was the smell of safety and security, and I knew it was not going to be there forever. OK, so that's not the real confession. That's pretty common among children as well as adults. The real confession is that I still find myself in CVS sniffing the jojoba body splash she used, and right there, for that moment, it brings her back. Maybe, at thirty years old, it is an odd thing to do, but it is *my* thing. I own it, and it never fails to bring me comfort.

We need to help grieving kids find their things that

they can own and that bring them comfort (and perhaps a strange look from fellow CVS shoppers now and then!).

A Kate's Club mom once shared that her ten-year-old daughter was having a very difficult time since losing her dad. Specifically, she was having a terrible time sleeping. An independent little girl, she had regressed, coming into her mom's bed every single night. This is a very common and understandable psychological reaction. So I drew on my own experience and gave her a simple tip. I told her that after my mom died, I kept a pair of her pajamas that I wore. I found that it brought me great comfort, and as a matter of fact, I still have them. So I suggested she do the same with one of her husband's T-shirts or nightshirts.

Giving your children a tangible way to keep a lost parent's memory in their minds and hearts is a great way of telling them that their grief is valid and real. And it doesn't have to be just clothing. Think of those things that are connected to your loved one. Did he love golf? You can pass on the clubs, or gloves, or golf balls. It could be a tennis racquet. Maybe pass along a music collection that meant a lot to the deceased parent and can form a connection with the child. Try and think of those things that your child can directly connect with the person. I have a friend who told me she has her mom's old dressing table and it brings her incredible comfort and memories. She can imagine her mom in that seat, her reflection in that mirror, an image and scene she has seen thousands of times before.

There are countless items you can choose from that can

serve as powerful connectors between your child and her loved one. But that is not to say all this is easy. I know from my experience with Kate's Club parents that holding on to memories can be a major hurdle. How do you navigate that line between honoring that person you have lost and memorializing them in a way that keeps you from truly moving forward? How do we determine what memories are healthy to share and which ones should remain private?

What it comes down to is a classic struggle between heart and head—waged at a time, unfortunately, when neither side is at its best. But don't let the enormity of this challenge scare you. Like so many other things in life, here is a situation where you must resist the temptation to do the easy thing instead of the right one.

Your parental instincts may tell you to protect your children from reminders of the person you have all lost. Maybe it's a way to protect yourself too. However, in doing so you would be missing an invaluable opportunity to strengthen your family. Your children's curiosity about the person they lost will only grow as they get older. By being open with them from an early age, you are putting down a solid foundation for that healing place we all need and deserve.

Embracing Them

When it comes to grief, memories are the ultimate investment. It's all about short-term pain and long-term gain. In those first days, weeks and months, there is nothing more painful than reminders of your enormous loss, especially as the lifelong repercussions are just starting to reveal themselves. It is totally understandable that your first instinct during this period is to erase memories rather than to embrace them.

You must remember this, however. Embracing these memories is going to help you create connections to a life and a person that are no longer physically accessible to you and your children. What follows are some conventional and unconventional ways to build those bridges.

The days and weeks after my mom's death were a whirlwind of activity. The thing I remember most is that it felt like there was a concerted effort to box up and remove all evidence of my mom and her life. Clothes were quickly sifted through and given away. Photos were taken down. Reminders were subtly removed until almost every remnant of our life as a complete family was safely tucked away in a box, or, worse, thrown away forever.

In order to avoid this situation, I encourage you to bring your child into the process of deciding how to handle your loved one's belongings. It can be a great way to bring the family together, and even to encourage positive memory sharing. Of course, this is all dependent on your individual child. I've said it many times: every grieving child is different. You may have a child who is clearly not ready or willing to participate in this process, and that is fine too. In this case, just be sure to set aside some memory items for later, as you will learn about farther on in this chapter. By sharing this experience with your kids, you are creating an opportunity to learn more about them and about some of the details of their grief journey that you may never have known otherwise.

I have heard many stories of experiences similar to my own. One day Mom or Dad was there and the next it was like that person never existed. The irony is that this protective strategy ends up causing far more harm than good. If the mere presence of that person in any form makes your life hard, choose a selfless route and think about the future— yours and your child's. Our memories answer great questions about our past and provide great clues about who we will eventually be, especially in the absence of a loved one who is no longer with us.

This is especially important for a child who is young enough to not be consciously aware of just who Mom or Dad was. Just because that person is no longer physically or mentally in that child's life does not mean he will not, or cannot, have a relationship with him or her in the future.

And the architect of the bridge to that relationship is you.

I have found that the healthiest grieving children I have encountered are the ones who have a real connection to both of the parents who brought them into this world. As children get older, they will become more and more interested in who and where they came from. It's just human nature to try and understand why we are who we are. This means you will likely get more questions from your child about your lost loved one, and as the thread that connects the two of them, it will be important for you to have answers.

One terrific way to do this is to start keeping a journal. This is always a great healing exercise in difficult times, but in this case it is doubly valuable in that it allows you to create a historical record of sorts that you and your children can go back to for many years to come.

Another excellent idea is to start keeping a scrapbook for your kids. This is a great way to balance keeping memories and treasures of your loved one accessible with the need to not overwhelm your family's search for a new identity as a unit. You and your child can visit this scrapbook whenever either of you wants to. In putting this book together, be conscious of your historian's role. Try to capture a comprehensive picture of the person as well as the life you shared together as a family. Use everything you can to paint this picture, from photographs, to cards or letters your loved one may have written, to condolence letters you may have received from family, friends and colleagues.

This is a perfect way not only to capture who that person was for your kids, but also to allow for that person's lessons and legacy to be a positive influence in your kids' lives. Here is also a chance for you to reach out to others who can contribute to this book and add new perspectives on the person you are capturing. Remember what we said about how uncomfortable people are with loss and grief? There are actually more people in your life than you know who would love to break through that discomfort and help. We'll talk a little more later in this chapter about how you can bring others in to help with other aspects of the grief journey, but here's a chance to introduce them to the process.

Start by asking people to share their recollections in a letter or email. See if they might have pictures or keepsakes that they would like to add to the book. You may find that your kids will find clues to themselves in these photos and memories, which makes the book an even greater treasure for all of you.

To take this activity one step further, you can build on this scrapbook and begin putting one together for your family after Mom or Dad has died. How does this help? Remember that while one life has ended, yours still continue to go on. Your lives, and your stories, are works in progress, and you have to recognize and honor that.

That is exactly what Debrah did.

Debrah's Scrapbook: Before and After

On the first anniversary of Melvin's death, Debrah took her kids for an overnight to Lake Lanier in Georgia. "I wanted them to remember that that was the day," she said, "and

I also wanted us all to get away. So we stayed in a nice hotel and we went swimming and had a great time. Later that evening I gave each child a photo album I had made just for them. It had pictures of their dad, but also of all the things we had done that year. I wanted them to look at it and say yes, we started here, but look at all the fun things we did this year. I told them they didn't need to look at it yet if they didn't feel like they were ready. But I know they did and I still see it on my son's night table sometimes."

I love the way she used memories to empower these kids. She made these memories tools that they could use however they wanted, and at times of their own choosing. At the same time she honored not only what they had been through in terms of their loss, but also what they had accomplished in the year following the loss. Debrah was making it clear to these kids that yes, they had lost, but they had also *lived*. What a valuable and powerful message!

At Kate's Club, we have done exercises where our kids bring in their favorite picture of their loved one who has died and create artwork or frames around this picture while sharing memories with one another about that person. A simple way you can translate this exercise at home is to have your children select one picture of Mom or Dad that carries significance and ask them to make a frame for it that you can display in the house. If your child is older and not so into the craft idea, it's enough to ask her to pick a picture for framing and let her choose a place to display it.

One of the things about the grief process for a young

person is that it wrests from them the little control they have over their lives, often at a time when they should be getting their first sense of how they fit into this world. When you do something like Debrah did here, you are giving some of that precious control back, and that can pay huge dividends in the future.

Storing Memories for Another Day

Sometimes with memories, as with everything else in life, timing is everything. You might find a perfect keepsake to pass along to your child but find that the child is too young to appreciate it. Here's where you need to use some foresight. Flash forward to the events to come in your child's life. Think of graduations, of weddings, of birthdays and other milestones . . . these are when your child will feel the absence of this person most acutely. You can help build the bridge that brings him to that moment.

That is what my dad did for me. On the day I graduated from high school, he gave me one of the best gifts I've ever received in my life. My mom only ever wore two rings, her engagement ring and her birthstone ring. Her birthstone was the same as mine. The stone was a peridot and the ring had two tiny diamonds on the side.

At my graduation party, my dad handed me a tiny box and I opened it to find the most beautiful ring. He had had the new ring arranged with the same stones placed in it, stones he had held on to just for me for six years, and given it to me on one of the most important days of my young life. Talk about your priceless treasures. I will always cherish that ring because of the importance these stones had in my mom's life, because they were given to me on such an important day in my life and because of the thought that went into my dad saving them. It brought her into my celebration in a way few other things could.

I remember a young boy coming to Kate's Club and proudly showing off his father's dog tags. Clearly, these were a symbol of his dad's life in the military and something that could allow the boy to express pride for and stay connected to his father.

How to Rely on the People Around You to Keep Memories Alive

These dog tags and my mom's ring are great examples of how a physical item can help you build those important bridges. But there are other more dynamic resources at your disposal as well. As we mentioned when talking about scrapbooks, there are plenty of people in your life who can help you and your kids remember the person you lost. You need to remember that there is a whole network of friends, family members, work colleagues and others who can give you perspective on your loved one you can never hope to have. Through their memories, their stories, their photos and perhaps their own keepsakes, they can provide a 360-degree picture of who this person was.

I urge you to look around your circle and identify those people who were close to your loved one and who can help remember that person in a healthy way. I am sure you have already found that there are times when your child may not be as open with you in sharing as you might like her to be. There are so many reasons for this, many of which we covered earlier. Your child may be afraid to dredge up too many sad things, as a way of protecting you. He may want to prove to you that he is strong himself. And it may have nothing to do with any of these things and merely be because at a certain age, kids get less comfortable talking with their parents about difficult emotions.

Whatever the reason, making sure that you include these other positive and safe influences in your kids' lives will provide a great outlet for both of you and can give you great peace of mind.

Never Too Late

Here's an important thing to remember when we are talking about enlisting the help of others: it is *never* too late.

As your kids get older, they will likely become more and more curious about not only the person they lost, but the whole family they left behind. This curiosity can be tied to important issues such as self-confidence and acceptance.

It certainly was for me. Even all these years after my mom's death, I am hungry for memories and stories that can fill in the many blanks I still have related to the relationship we had. The loss of the love I so coveted from my mom left a huge hole in my life. So in the past few years I have reached out to a number of people to seek their help. What I found was that now, after nearly twenty years, people are more than happy to share their memories. It was almost as if the process helped them to find their own voices after all this time.

One of the people I reached out to was my aunt. She shared stories of her visits to Charlottesville when I was a little girl, and memories of our family that I will cherish forever. If you can imagine my emotional satisfaction when I received the following note, you can see how powerful such transcripts can be to bring peace and healing to your child's life.

Dear Kate,

When I made it to C-Ville, a whole new chapter in my life started. I walked in and found this immensely engaging girl-child . . . who was sorta like having a July 4th sparkler going off in your house all the time. You were so cute and funny, full of energy, always laughing. I do honestly believe that you were a tremendous relief and sense of enjoyment for your parents.

On one of these visits, I saw you do the cutest thing for the first time. We (your mom and I) were laughing with you and you got up and went over to your mother. She was sitting on the couch . . . you got up beside her on your knees so you were just high enough to get your arm around

*her shoulder and she would put her arm around you. It was
such a cute, sweet thing for a child to do, and I could see it
gave your mother great pleasure.*

*You were a treat. Just an amazing pleasure to your par-
ents. You easily gave love . . . and so it was very easy to
love you.*

I will never be able to thank my aunt enough for this
short note, or for the flurry of additional correspondence it
inspired. She painted a picture I would never otherwise have
been able to see. She illustrated the reality of my mother's
love, a force I have been craving since the day she left this
earth. And all it took was a few minutes at a computer.

Erasing Them: A Child's Biggest Fear

The above example proves how important sharing memories can be with grieving kids, even years after the loss.
However, the process of helping your child with these
memories begins immediately. Remember that you are the
one in charge of how these memories are handled. And one
of your most important roles is to avoid the perception that
you are trying to erase memories of your loved one from
your home and from your life.

I know from my own experience and the experiences
of my Kate's Club kids that this breeds a feeling of distrust.
And nothing puts cracks in the foundation of your healing
place like distrust can.

It's easy to lose sight of the impact the loss of a loved one has on a young person's life when we're caught up in our own personal struggles with the loss. As we've said, the death of a family member punctures that protective bubble of innocence that is the very essence of childhood. It shows them that parents can die. That life can be arbitrary and horribly unfair. And on top of that, it is a child's first sign of her own mortality.

One of the most terrifying things to a child is the idea that he could be forgotten. After all, if children watch the memory of Mom or Dad fade away, who is to say that the memories of them won't fade just as quickly? In dealing with death for the first time, a child really starts to think about life for the first time. Most likely before this, your child's innocence bubble has kept her from really developing a big picture about life. This of course depends on age, and on your family's faith and table conversation around life. But often it takes a jolt as sudden as losing a parent for these thoughts to really hit home.

I remember doing one activity with the kids at Kate's Club where we made graffiti posters. The kids were all given poster boards as their canvas, and they had to select one feeling associated with their grief that was the most prevalent for them since their loved one had died. They were asked to do a poster around this emotion, using text or images or anything they thought best communicated this feeling. After the children were done, they went around to the other posters, and whenever they came upon an emotion they felt they shared with a peer, they autographed that poster.

The exercise was a great example of the power of common ground when it comes to peer interaction. But there was one poster in particular that got my attention. The theme for this poster, inked by a young gal who had lost her older sister, was "Forgotten." As we discussed the posters, she shared that she was not only scared of forgetting her sister as years passed, but also that she too would be forgotten when she died. I thought this was such a mature idea for a middle-school-age child, and it reminded me of just how significant this fear is among children who experience death early in life.

Having strong memories, and the confidence to share those memories with others, helps kids find a purpose not only in their grief, but in their life. We all want to be significant, especially to those we love the most. So work on providing healthy ways to honor and remember your loved one, as it becomes such an important tool for your grieving child.

Memories take a vital role in building your healing place. They can empower and unite your family and, most important, create a comfort within your home around the idea that grief is a part of your family's story, but not the ending. Memories can fuel your child's voice and the emotions that are necessary to move forward in the grief process.

Don't shy away from these memories, but rather embrace and use them to build a healing home that continues to be a loving, safe place for your child to grieve and to live. Using memories as tools can help your child both express sadness, which we discussed earlier as a healthy reaction to grief, and also reconnect them to laughter, an important force for healing that we will discuss in the next chapter.

CHAPTER SIX

Tears and Laughter:
Both Are Essential

One of my favorite quotes comes from the great psychiatrist Carl Jung. He said, "Even a happy life cannot be balanced without a measure of darkness, and the word happy would lose its meaning if it were not balanced by sadness."

This is a quote that perfectly captures one of my core principles concerning grief. You *must* balance your sadness with your happiness. They may seem like the two extremes of emotional expression, but as grieving people we live between them. And as with any other human being, our moods, our thoughts and the events in our lives regularly move us toward one extreme or the other. Your healing place will be made stronger by the healthy presence of both laughter and tears.

Sadness Is Not a Four-Letter Word

Let's start with sadness. It's the first, overwhelming emotion you dealt with around your loss. If we are going to talk about emoting and communicating honestly about grief, we are going to be talking about sadness. It will be a major part of your grief throughout its lifelong existence. It just doesn't always have to be the only part.

Our culture has a strange relationship with sadness. On one level, we are drawn to it in the worlds of entertainment, or even news. Tearjerker movies still pack theaters and fly off the rental shelves. And even in a time when attention spans are shrinking by the minute, news stories of loss and grief can still pull huge ratings and readership for days and weeks on end.

Yet when that sadness is transferred to our real world, when it penetrates the protective bubbles of our own lives, we are conditioned to run.

We are missing a very basic point here. Not only is there nothing wrong with sadness, it is a key ingredient in our healing process. It's like all those foods that are regularly put on the "Do Not Eat" list by nutritional experts. Sadness can be incredibly healthy when experienced in moderation. By suppressing our sadness, we almost guarantee that it will seep, and even burst out, in most unhealthy ways.

It's the same thing we have done with germs. Our

culture is so germ-phobic that many medical experts think that overdoing preventive measures has left us increasingly unable to handle what used to be rather simple threats to our health. Some see evidence of it in the number of dangerous childhood allergies present in our kids today.

In the same way, we are running the risk of equally dangerous consequences when we shelter our kids from sadness. We need sadness. We need to face it, even to embrace it, and to recognize it for the balance it provides in our lives. Instead, we tend to replace conversations and realizations with medications. We accept the message of moderation in so many other areas of our life, from money to food to health. Yet when it comes to emotions, we are taught that any public expression of sadness risks our being labeled unstable.

I am sure that you are used to seeing and dealing with sadness in your children. How you deal with it, I would guess, has a lot to do with where it comes from. For instance, it is fairly easy to counsel a child whose sadness is misplaced, or comes from a place that, in the big picture, might not merit such a reaction. Here's an example. If your child is in the throes of a first heartbreak, you are probably going to be supportive. Yet you will also know that this is a sort of typical life event that she has to go through and you may spend some of your time convincing her that perhaps it is not so sad a situation after all. In the end, though, you are probably going to know in your heart that your child will be OK. Certainly a first-crush heartbreak is a much less intense life experience than losing a mom or dad.

But what really makes the grief scenerio different from any other child-rearing lesson is that you share it. And while you know by now that your child can't be "fixed," you still may have to fight that instinct to cut off the reaction and make it all better. You need to learn that while tears hurt, they also heal.

Giving the OK to Cry

Just as with so many things we have talked about, this is another great opportunity to set the course for your family's grief journey. Your main goal, remember, is to create a healing place, to establish that comfort zone where the pressures and unwritten rules in the rest of society do not apply.

We have talked about the importance of letting your child see you express your emotions. We all cry, and your child needs to feel completely validated in doing so himself. Your child can cry openly in front of you or behind closed doors. In either case, it is very important that you support her need to do so.

This is not always easy to do. No matter how in tune you are with each other's emotions or how close you have become after your loss, there is no synchronization capability on our emotional clocks. You might find yourself in a whole different head space when your child is breaking down. It's another responsibility on your shoulders. You need to allow him to let it go and let it flow.

Let me also mention, though, that some children will choose not to cry. And that's OK too. Denial is a normal reaction to grief and may not always come right at the beginning. Denial may be brought on because a child feels limits on how she is able to express her grief. Perhaps she doesn't want to cry, but feels that a better way to express herself is through laughter. This is OK too, and that's the reason I mention these two expressions in one breath, as contrasting as they may seem.

Tears and Laughter: The Bridge of Expression

The spectrum of expression is wide, and your child needs to feel comfortable all throughout it.

To me, I look at the expression of emotions as a bridge, one that you can walk back and forth on and stop along the way when you need to. To stop on this bridge is to be present and to express openly how you are feeling, so that those emotions don't get jammed. Think about the times in your life when you have really cried, in grief but also outside of and even before your loss. I hope that in many of those times you were fortunate to have a caring shoulder for the tears to fall on and a caring heart to take in your sorrow and provide you the support you needed.

When I think about those times for me, I'm amazed

by how often they were immediately followed by laughter. There is just something about letting your emotions out, whichever extreme you happen to be expressing, that is cleansing. It's like your tears have cleared the path for laughter to follow, until sometimes they become intertwined and you don't know if you are in fact laughing or crying!

So I urge you to recognize that even in the midst of tears, you may ultimately find laughter, and to remember that one can be as healing as the other! With your child, keeping the landscape open to express both sadness and joy is your best recipe. Just by telling your kids it's OK to laugh and OK to cry gives him control of this expression and relief to choose his own path to do so. This is the first step in creating this environment in your healing home.

Keeping Laughter Alive

It's up to us as adults to make sure we help our kids with this reconnecting process. But how?

First, you have to commit to rediscovering laughter for yourself. Go beyond giving your child the permission to laugh. Give *yourself* the permission to laugh. It might seem like something you'd never in your life have to be given permission to do, but for many this is a necessary step. Never underestimate the power of guilt to take from us those things we want and need. Laughter can fall into this category, especially in the early days of loss.

Know this. Recognize this. And make the decision to push through and accept laughter's healing qualities. Once you have done this for yourself, you can better do the same for your kids. It's right back to the oxygen mask example.

Be conscious of creating situations where laughter can occur, or taking advantage of those situations when they appear. When you see that laughter door open even just a crack, throw it wide open and run through it together with your child. You will soon see, I think, that you are doing much more than helping your child. You are also giving yourself an invitation to return to that childlike innocence we all need to visit from time to time.

Sit down and watch a completely silly movie. Indulge your kids in bouts of pure nuttiness. Do whatever it takes to connect with your child's innate need for and appreciation of joy. Take advantage of laughter's contagious quality. Is there anything better in life than those moments when a group of people gets laughing so hard that in the end they are not even sure what they were laughing about in the first place?

Laughter's power is not reserved for building a healthy soul. No less an expert than Sigmund Freud wrote of its larger healing powers. His "Relief Theory of Laughter" explains how laughter releases tension and is thus beneficial to one's health, and why it is thus a great coping mechanism when one is angry or sad.

Dr. Freud is hardly alone in touting these physiological

benefits. According to a number of studies from leading hospitals around the world, laughter has some important and legitimate health benefits as well. A 2008 study by cardiologists at the University of Maryland Medical Center in Baltimore indicated that laughter may actually help prevent heart disease. They polled three hundred people. The groups were dividied in half, the first group including people who had suffered heart attacks or undergone coronary bypass surgery and the second including people with healthy hearts. What the doctors found was that the first group, according to Michael Miller, MD, director of the Center for Preventive Cardiology at the medical center and associate professor at the University of Maryland School of Medicine, "responded less humorously to everyday life situations. They generally laughed less, even in positive situations, and they displayed more anger and hostility."

Though this example skews more to the well-being of one's physical body, it also shows you how our mental and physical health are so closely tied together. It tells us that laughter can have a lasting effect on our grief recovery and our ability to move on in a positive way.

The greatest thing about laughter as a tool in your healing place is that you will never run out of it. It's at your disposal all the time. That is something I taught myself very early on in my journey. I told myself at a very early age that any day that did not include laughter would represent failure for me. Anyone who knows me well will tell you the same thing. For me, it's part of choosing that survivor route. I refused to let what happen to me cut me off from something that is such an essential part of life. I mentioned earlier that children seek out a simple path in their grief as in their lives: the path of most hope. I hope you will see that laughter is an essential fuel to carry you and your family along your respective and collective paths.

Seeking Out Laughter

Remember when, at the beginning of this chapter, I mentioned how special times can reconnect your family to the joy and laughter you experienced before Mom or Dad died? Let's look at how we can reclaim these times during intense times of grief. There are special times at Kate's Club when we get to take our kids and their families to really neat activities that are happening around Atlanta. One year, Cirque du Soleil gave Kate's Club several free tickets to offer to our families. I always enjoy being able to provide such an activity to our parents, an unexpected surprise, a gift of time to spend together with their kids that was not planned in their daily struggles with their grief. One note we received from a mom after she saw the circus stated it all. She wrote, "Our family will remember this event for a long time. It was so nice to smile, clap, laugh, be in awe, etc, feelings that we sometimes otherwise take for granted (and I used to), come so much harder when you've lost such a close loved one."

The reason this is important, like the act itself, is simple. Laughter is about restoring two of the most precious gifts grieving children can be given: hope and optimism.

Kate's Club is founded on four pillars: fun, safety, community and long-term. It is no accident that "fun" is the first one listed. Who can think of children without thinking of fun and laughter? Even more important, there is nothing that kids universally relate to like laughter and fun. Just because the grief door has opened in these young lives doesn't mean that fun and joy need to leave through it. These two elements are essential to the grief process for all ages, but particularly so for those young minds and hearts that are unable to vocalize their feelings around what has happened to them.

The Role of Child's Play

The night my mom died, I walked into my parents' room and asked my dad if it was OK to go out and play with my friends. On other days I wouldn't have asked permission in such a "guilt-filled" way, but that was no ordinary day. I remember feeling guilty about seeking fun and play with my friends, but at the same time, it was all I wanted to do that day. I didn't want to stay in the house, with all those people, dealing with their careful and concerned observation of my every move. While the intentions behind my concern were good, it did nothing for me in that moment but build anxiety and discomfort. What I really needed was to get out of there and be with my friends. It felt strange to me at the time, but I now know the reaction was completely normal.

Obviously, I needed an escape hatch, and what child in that situation wouldn't? But I later realized that I also needed something even more basic and powerful: I needed to connect to the childlike innocence I was already worried had disappeared forever.

My friends really helped me remain grounded and feel connected to that safe, fun life I'd had before my mom died. Their simple support, even though we were too young to ever really talk about death and grief, was something I now recognize as a very important stage of my healing process.

When it came time for me to start Kate's Club, it should come as no surprise that the first program was created entirely around building friendships similar to the ones that had kept me going. But with one special element that I always wished I'd had: a friend who shared my experience of loss. That was the golden ticket and that was what made Kate's Club special from Day 1. Our club outing program features monthly adventures to various places throughout Atlanta, from sporting events to museums to theaters, arcades and more. The recipe was simple: fun and friendship meant comfort. Comfort meant sharing. And sharing meant healing. Even without the guided facilitation of a therapist, these kids immediately formed incredible bonds of friendship that freed them up to talk, laugh and share in ways they never had before. I recall many rides in that shuttle van where the first question asked was "So, who did you lose?"—yes, that was even more direct than I had expected. But I don't recall one time a child shied away from answering the question, not among those peers.

These kids proved what I had always suspected: that there is as much healing from grief with fun as there is with sadness. Kids often describe Kate's Club as fun, and that is a measure of success for us. Not that grief is fun. There is nothing fun about losing someone you loved too early in life. But the connection to fun and laughter and joy while grieving is one of the most motivating tools in healthy healing.

Laughter as Grief's Best Medicine

Anyone who has heard a child's unbridled laugh can tell you it is one of life's absolute joys. It is also one of life's absolute necessities. It is no accident that laughter is called "the best medicine." For a grieving child, it is even more than that. Laughter can become a way back to the innocence she may have thought she'd lost forever. Kids in this situation need to be connected again with the things that define them as kids. And nothing does this quite like laughter and fun.

When my dad gave me that OK to laugh, he was not only relieving me of some guilt I was feeling, he was teaching me a life lesson that is at the core of who I am—that no matter the circumstances, we all have the capability of laughter to relieve the pressure and help us on the road to recovery.

In my own way, I made Kate's Club about saying yes to this unspoken question from every child who walks through our doors. Ask any of our kids to describe what Kate's Club means to them, and I can pretty much guarantee you "fun" will be in the first sentence or two. I can usually see some hesitation in kids the first time they walk through our doors. It's like they are not sure if it is really OK to be having this much fun. Yet they learn by example, from their peers, that it is more than OK. It is what they are expected to do!

Kate's Club kids laugh because they can. They laugh because they are in an environment that feels safe and welcoming, where they are seen for who they truly are rather than merely for who they are in the wake of what has happened to them.

As with everything else in this book, I want you to learn how to translate this approach to your own home. It all goes back to not making the process of helping your children harder than it needs to be. Laughter is the simplest tool of all, and that is a good thing. Don't get caught up thinking that in creating your healing place, there always has to be a clinical dynamic in the room. What you are really looking for is connections, and nothing connects people quite like laughter does. You can encourage this at home by creating fun experiences as a family and encouraging your child to engage in fun activites among peers.

Laughter Breaks Down Walls

What I think you will find is that these laughter connections can lead to much more important moments. Fun and laughter can lead to meaningful and healing conversations. By lightening the load just for those moments, you might be able to get past those things that have been blocking you or weighing you down. I urge you to take advantage of these light moments to connect around the memory of your loved one. Go ahead and tell a story that involves funny memories with that person. You might find that sharing these kinds of memories with your child can open up new levels of honesty, empowering her and you to talk more openly about how much you both miss the loved one you lost.

Laughter's Lasting Bonds

I think you will find that the benefits of sharing laughter extend far beyond the wonderful sounds of the giggles and the guffaws. And that these benefits can bond you together with your child not just in his early years, but throughout your lives.

Here's a great example. I recently was told a story by a young woman who lost her dad when she was in college. Though legally an adult, she still felt it was premature for him to die. She and her mother had this great adventure taking her dad's cremated ashes to his birthplace in Georgia. It was a full day's drive, and they planned on staying at a hotel, then getting up early to spread his ashes. As they entered the hotel, the desk clerk asked the two of them, "How many?" This young woman tells this story because it was the first time she laughed after her dad died. She and her mom exchanged a glance, not knowing how to respond to the question. I mean, do they count Dad or not? So they both just released this laughter—and she said it was such a relief to restore that feeling of happiness and joy in her life, even for that brief moment and (somewhat) at her father's expense.

I love this story because it illustrates one of the qualities that defines us as human beings. We have the power to use our minds and hearts to find the ironic, the absurd and the just plain silly in even the most serious of situations.

Tears and Laughter: Keeping It Simple

Not too long ago I appeared on CNN along with a young Kate's Club member. The interviewer asked what advice I would give a young person who had lost a parent. Nothing like being asked to encapsulate years' worth of lessons in a thirty-second sound bite!

But I tried. I started to talk in adult terms. My answers were complex. I was looking to highlight my professionalism and showcase my credentials. Leave it up to the adult in me to assume that complexity would serve as a sign of achievement.

What I failed to recognize and what I hope you learn in this book is that we all need continually to remind ourselves of the power of simplicity in life, even when coping with the deep pain and heartache associated with loss.

This power was not lost on my young Kate's Club friend. When he was asked the same question, his answer contained no cerebral analysis about the complicated implications of grief. He said things like "it will be hard" and "you can cry." He also told them, "You have to keep on living."

I sat there proud and amazed at the message he was able to share. It resonated with me far more than my own had. He went on to say, "You should let it out, and if you feel that you need to keep it in, you should keep it in. All these feelings are natural."

It's not hard to look back now and see which one of us the audience connected with most.

What he said that day captures what I feel about laughter as much as it does what I feel about tears—and everything in between. Emotions are a part of life. Looked at in this light, you come to understand that all emotions are good emotions. This is a powerful lesson to teach your kids, especially in this time of loss.

Yes, it's OK to laugh. Yes, it's OK to cry. Yes, it's OK to be happy. Yes, it's OK to be sad. Yes, it's OK to be angry. And maybe most important of all, yes, it's OK to look behind, but it's even more important to look ahead.

We can all help these kids to understand this. One way

is by making it clear that while a life has ended, their lives have just begun. And while grief will always be a part of their lives, it does not have to rule them. Remember that when you feel overwhelmed, your child probably does as well. Remind yourself and your family to keep life simple, don't try to do too much. Be patient with yourself and with your kids.

Laugh. Cry. Love. Live. Repeat!

CHAPTER SEVEN

Change Happens:
Handling Traditions and Transitions

Although the term "grief" is often used to refer to the sense of loss following a death, it in fact by definition refers to the reaction to any loss or change. We've spent a lot of time working on helping you build a healing place in your home. Now we're going to look at how you can maintain it and keep your family healthy and connected as you move through your journey.

Remember that your family's grief will not end. You all will grieve and re-grieve your loss, all at different times and different places, for the rest of your lives. The most common triggers of your grief in a given year may include holidays and other milestones in the grief journey, such as birthdays, anniversaries, etc. They will also likely include transitions such as your child's return to school.

Navigating change of any kind is one of life's biggest challenges. But with the right perspective and outlook, it can be one of life's biggest opportunities. It is no surprise that changes to routines and traditions are particularly difficult for grieving children. They have had a change forced upon them that no one could ever want.

People often make the mistake of putting a timetable on kids' grief because kids focus on the day-to-day, giving little thought to the future or the past. This can make adults feel that their child's healing process is somehow accelerated. Please be careful with assumptions like these. The effect of loss on grieving kids is systemic, reaching into every part—their hearts, their minds and their souls.

Just because a child may not be showing the kind of reaction you might expect after a loss, it doesn't mean she has super healing powers. Just when you think you have a child's grief pattern figured out, it can change. It's easy to assume your child is just learning how to move on. But a more likely explanation is that he is creating some comfortable space and his own timeline to begin to process this enormous loss in his life.

And guess what may jolt your child out of this comfortable space and trigger that initial, and sometimes explosive, expression of grief? Another change. It can be a move, a change in the classroom, a natural change in the child's development (such as puberty). Every childhood change can be difficult for a developing boy or girl. You can at least double that difficulty for a grieving child. And the changes that trigger a grief response can happen once or many times over a period of years.

Your child lives life by an annual plan. Autumn means school. November and December mean holiday traditions. Spring usually brings about sports and spring break. Summer may mean a family vacation. Changes to any of these routines hit grieving kids particularly hard.

This sense of routine is literally born into every child. Most parents will tell you that routines are the key to happiness in their infants—giving them a sense of order that these tiny creatures crave. When a child experiences something such as losing a parent, a core disruption of that child's routine and daily life both mentally and physically, any other change can then play an integral part in how and when the child grieves. So just be aware of this and don't question it. The reactions to these changes will likely vary based on age. Your older child, for instance, may feel shame around being disturbed by what might seem to most to be a small transition. Your younger child may not be able to put into words at all exactly why she is disturbed.

In those first days, weeks and months after a loss, there is a lot of attention on a grieving child. It's common to hear the story of a house flooded with family and friends, and too much food, in the days after a loved one dies. This care and attention extended to children is present and is important. But it suddenly goes away just a few weeks after, with, yes, much relief, but also with seeming reckless abandon.

Perhaps this is also where your journey begins as a grieving parent. Suddenly the activity stops and you are now alone as a family again. Your eyes now become an important tool as you begin to take stock of your child's evolving grief. Grief isn't transactional, so when the public stops acknowledging it, it doesn't mean it is over. I don't have to tell you that. But unfortunately, after the obituaries are published and the funeral is held, most of those around you will close out that experience and move forward with their lives, far from the pain of the daily grief that you and your family will continue to feel. Yours really is just beginning, so don't let your child get confused and feel that those feelings should end because the outside public isn't paying attention.

While some approach grief in stages, there is no time-line and there isn't necessarily a set progression through these stages. According to Harvard's Child Bereavement Study, many children are more at risk for emotional and behavioral difficulties two years after a death than they were immediately after or at one year after the death. More children feel fearful or anxious even a year after the death than right away. And two years after the death, many bereaved children in the study reported lower self-worth than non-bereaved children.

Triggers

I commonly use the word "triggers" when talking about grief. Triggers are events that intensify one's grief, and they happen throughout life. A healthy person works to acknowledge and understand the events and the times at which triggers may occur. I certainly have a better understanding of these triggers as an adult and as someone who has studied the grief experience. But I didn't always have this knowledge. As I've shared, my transition to college life was a huge time of intense grief for me. It had been eight years since my mom passed away. But that bundle of changes, including academic adjustments, meeting a vast new array of people, adjusting to a new form of independence . . . it all brought on an enormous amount of sadness. Most of all, it made me miss my maternal safety net in a way that nothing had up to that point.

Going off to college is a huge life change for any child, but for me, my grief compounded that experience and made it tremendously challenging. Though I was able to move through this intense time and come out OK, I certainly could have had a better time with it had I been more prepared for the change. Your child might not be ready to head off to college yet, but he is certainly always looking toward big changes in his life. Your children are, after all, kids. And they have a long list of milestones to experience.

Let's talk about some of those changes and triggers and how you can help support your child through them. Being prepared for them will allow you to be more available to your child and thus maintain the healing environment within the home.

The First Day Back at School . . .
Returning to the Classroom After a Loss

If a parent dies during a school year, it clearly causes an abrupt absence from your child's normal routine. One of the first encounters with anxiety in your child's grief may be around her return to school. It's difficult to identify the "right" time for your child to return to school, and you won't find prescriptive research on a timeline. Every child is different, and you need to work with your child to find the right timetable. This is a good time to begin engaging your child in decisions related to his grief journey. Allow him to decide when the time is right to start back at school.

For me, at twelve years old, I remember being very anxious to return to school after my mom died. Looking back now, I know I was yearning for a sense of routine and an environment that wasn't as emotionally overwhelming as my home was. The enormity of my mother's death was simply something I could not grasp at that age. I wanted to get back with my peers. I wanted a sense of normalcy in a life that had been robbed of it in every other way. I wanted to be able to comprehend and interact on levels that I understood.

In most cases, a child's desire to return to a routine has nothing to do with bouncing back. It has everything to do with the fact that the child is far from ready to begin to process what is happening to him, so he's looking for something familiar to fall back into . . . . . something that reminds him of the comfort of his now "former" life.

While I quickly reengaged, my fourteen-year-old brother took a little longer to want to go back, for reasons that were personal to him. This is an example of the importance of honoring your children with different timetables.

The key here, as in so many issues with grieving children, is communication. Don't allow the conversation about returning to school be limited to a daily yes/no check-in. If the answer is no and continues to be no, use that as an opportunity to dig a little deeper and see if you can get to the root of the reluctance. It is very likely there is more going on that just can't be left to assumptions.

Though I hesitate to classify any individual in the grief process, it is safe to say that age plays a role in this decision. Older kids are able to process such events in a way younger kids often cannot. An older kid generally has a greater ability and tendency to anticipate her return to school, and anxiety may build as a result of that. Younger kids, at a different cognitive stage of their development, lack this capacity and thus are often not as burdened by this anxiety.

For any school-age child, make sure that when the decision is made to return, the support nets are up. This means keeping the dialogue open with your kids throughout these first few days and weeks back. Make sure you carve out some time in the afternoons and evenings to talk to your child about how this important transition is going for them.

This is another great example of how you can use communication to smooth your child's path through a major transition and potential grief trigger.

How to Reach Out to Your School

In addition to this communication with your child, I recommend you engage your child's teacher and/or guidance counselor in this transition and return to school. These are two key individuals in your child's life. And while they are likely already aware of the death, checking in with them can greatly help you extend your healing environment from home to school. Part of anticipating any triggers is helping your child's environment to be prepared as well. For kids, school is a big one.

Unfortunately, you can't assume that your child's teacher or guidance counselor will be prepared to address his new challenges. I, along with other staff members at Kate's Club, have often talked to school administrators and teachers who are looking to educate themselves on how to help their students who are dealing with grief. This is a great sign, but we still have a long way to go toward a true understanding and acceptance of the issues grieving students face. That is why I urge you to take the initiative and directly bring these people into your child's support network. Don't underestimate the importance of this growing network. Your role as your child's advocate has expanded. With this added responsibility comes added pressure. Don't try to handle it all alone! The more people there are in this circle who can truly understand your child's new challenges, the easier it will be for you to help your child find peace and healing.

The repercussions of loss will hit your child in many different ways, some visible and some not. For instance, it is not at all uncommon for grieving kids to struggle with academics, even if it is an area where they have never struggled before. This can be upsetting and frustrating for parents, and it adds significant stress to an already stressful situation. The same goes for changes in social habits. Sometimes an outgoing child can withdraw, or a child can veer into dangerous social territory that was completely uncharacteristic of her up until the loss occurred.

By engaging your school community, you are adding eyes and ears to your network and giving yourself a better chance of staying on top of those aspects of your child's life that you can't possibly follow and manage by yourself.

So how can you best do this? First, if possible, join your child on his first day back at school. This is especially important for younger kids. Ask if you can spend five minutes with the teacher. Do the same with the guidance counselor. In these conversations, be open and honest. Let them know that you aren't looking for your child to be treated differently, but just want the teacher and you to have open communication in the coming months. Let the teacher and/or guidance counselor know that you are available and would like to know how your child is reacting to this transition back to school.

I also strongly recommend setting up an outlet for your child with the guidance staff and your child's teacher. Set up an agreement that if your child feels overwhelmed or needs an outlet from the classroom, she is safe to go sit in the guidance office. This is a great way to ease the child's return to school. The guidance staff is qualified to assess and support your child on a one-to-one basis, rather than the teacher having to take his or her focus off the rest of the class. None of this is complicated. It's about creating an honest and open pipeline of communication, which you know by now is a key to all your grief journey success. What you are doing is giving your child options, which every child wants and needs—especially when in unfamiliar territory. And no territory for a child is more unfamiliar than grief.

For older kids, I would still visit the school, although most likely a high-schooler wouldn't appreciate you walking in there with him. So place a phone call or set up a time to come in and talk to a teacher and/or guidance counselor. I have seen this same outlet arrangement work for high-schoolers as well as younger kids. As with any option, kids can test boundaries at times, so make sure your child isn't abusing the arrangement. Rely on your guidance counselor and/or teacher to help make sure this isn't the case.

I have also heard of teachers sharing their own personal

stories of loss with a child. This can help make the class-room a healing place as well. So if a teacher shares a story like this with you, encourage him or her to do the same with your child. Encouraging others to share in this way is an important part of extending your child's healing environment outside of your home.

A New School Year: New Faces, New Studies and New Grief

As I've mentioned, all transitions can be landmines for grieving kids. Perhaps the most predictable of the transitions are new classes and new schools. Changes like these have a unique way of dredging up all kinds of fears and worries, even for kids who seemed to thrive in their previous classrooms. They established a foundation of support to help manage their grief in their previous setting. Now moving to a new class requires them to start the process all over again. This will often trigger a response that can play out both academically and socially.

This is a prime opportunity for you to communicate with your child. The three key things to convey to her are:

1. Starting a new year/new school can be tough. It's OK to be struggling a little bit with this change. It's OK if it brings up sad feelings related to Mom/Dad.

2. I'm here for you.

3. I did talk to your new teacher and let him or her know
about our loss. If you need any support while at school,
your teacher and guidance staff are there for you too.

Let your child know that you are available to him even
when you are not physically there, and that there are others
who are invested in him and available as well. Even if your
child shrugs off the need for support, as a typical preteen
or teen may, know that you are still making her aware of a
comfort zone that is available to her.

When Kate's Club dad Norman was getting ready to
send his daughter Sarah Ann to a new school, he did all this
and more. He was facing a particularly difficult situation
in that Sarah Ann's mom died one week before the start of
middle school. While there is *never* a good time to lose a
parent, I can't think of a worse time than on the verge of
what is probably the toughest school transition of all. And
remember that this little girl had much more than that on
her plate. She was also adjusting to having to move to a
new city to live with her dad, who had been divorced from
her mom for nearly five years at that point. Taking all this
into consideration like the incredible dad he is, Norman
took the proactive route.

"I went to the school's open house that first week and sat
down with each one of her teachers. I found out who they
were, I talked to them about what had transpired. I just
wanted to make sure they knew ahead of time."

Norman didn't stop there. "I think it is of the utmost

importance to check in with teachers at regular intervals," he said, "just to see how things are progressing. Is she being quiet? Any outbursts? Is she talking back? I think it is important for the surviving parent of any child to be mindful of this when their child is in school. It is important to check in on the emotional piece. I let them know that if they saw certain emotions, lots of daydreaming, or anything that seemed out of the ordinary in the classroom I wanted them to keep me abreast of that."

This is a great thing to do, because the more information you have, the better you are able to decide how you want to deal with your child about these issues. Or if you even need to. It's hard for a surviving parent to gauge behavior sometimes, because you are continually dealing with your child's emotions. You may get the brunt of things much more than another authority figure would. But if you learn that there are behaviors of concern that are translating to the classroom, you can use that information to approach the situation with your child. For instance, if you hear there are frequent outbursts or talking back, or if you hear your child is retreating into silence in a way that could affect academic performance and social life, you can feel empowered to start a dialogue around it with your child.

Norman used this approach to reach out beyond Sarah Ann's classroom teachers. "I made sure that I talked to the teachers, to the principals, the counselors, the head counselor for our county's school system . . . anybody I could talk to who had an influence on Sarah Ann being successful that year at school."

This is a great example of a parent taking a proactive approach to an often difficult situation. Norman was not in there asking for special treatment. He was giving these teachers, counselors and administrators a full picture of who his daughter was and the possible challenges she might face. And he was establishing a network for himself of people who could give him valuable information on the important parts of her grief journey that he could not see firsthand.

Even in these difficult times, Norman never lost sight of the goal we all have when it comes to helping grieving kids: we're trying to help these kids *live with* grief as opposed to being ruled by it. And if that means you need to reach out to teachers for a beginning-of-the-year conversation for several years after a loss, it is well worth the effort in the long run.

The same is true for athletic and social organizations. Being part of a team can be such a positive experience for kids who have experienced loss. At the same time, however, the equipment will be put away at season's end and your child will be looking at a brand-new team when the next year begins. Recognize this by talking about it with your child, but also take a minute to pull the coach aside and let him or her know that there may be change-related issues.

Whether we are talking about teachers or coaches,

I have had many parents express concern that they will be seen as asking for special treatment for their children. That couldn't be farther from the truth. What you are doing is helping your child and providing an important service to the teacher and the school.

Remember that you aren't asking this person to take any sort of action. The goal is just to offer awareness. By being aware, these people can help you extend a heathly environment for your child to move forward and ultimately turn his loss into an opportunity to thrive. Children thrive when and where they feel safe. Communicating with the influential adults in your child's life will help to create that safe, emotional space for her.

At Kate's Club this is a primary role of the buddies. They don't probe for conversations or force any communication, but they are influential adults in our members' lives who are aware and supportive of their grief, thus creating a space for the kids to focus on moving forward and reaching their goals and dreams.

Whether you realize it now or not, you have buddies all around you. Your child's teachers, counselors, coaches, babysitters . . . these can all play the same role our Kate's Club buddies play for our kids. Use the adults who spend quality time with your child as a support network. It doesn't take much from them or from you. It just takes communication. Make it comfortable and simple. These are the places that your child associated mostly with life—the school, the playing field, the playground. These are places they should still associate childhood with. Your job is just to lay some extra cushions down for their emotional safety, so that they can reengage in a healthy and happy way.

The school return is a transition that happens early in your child's grief journey. Though larger events such as graduation and starting college may bring about a trigger farther down the line, for the most part, this is an event to prepare for in the short-term at the beginning of your child's grief. Now we'll move into some other times and events—i.e., trigger points—in your life that need extra care and attention on your part to support your child.

The Dreaded First-Year Anniversary

Many families have great anxiety around the calendar in the first year after a loss. Every time a new month appears, it brings so many reminders of your loved one and the new and unwanted life you now face as a family. It's only natural to face each new day with a range of reminders as you try to find your footing without this person in your lives. We all go through it. The first year is filled with firsts—from birthdays to anniversaries. The anticipation around these significant days is enough to paralyze even the healthiest of grieving families. I encourage you to take a lot of deep breaths this first year.

One of the biggest hurdles can be the first anniversary

of a loved one's actual death. It is perfectly normal for there to be heightened anxiety around this event. As this date approaches, be open in your communication. Talk about what the day means to you, and engage your kids in conversations about how it makes them feel.

My advice? Make this day a celebration. Yes, there is great sadness around the day and that will always be there. But there is also an opportunity for empowerment. When you truly celebrate the person you lost, you celebrate everything about him or her, including the joy you experienced in the times you spent together.

It's all about reclaiming your stake to that cherished Trophy of Love. Remember what Debrah did with that scrapbook: acknowledge the day and the loss, but also celebrate your Trophies and celebrate the new family you have become and the stability that you have created even in the face of tragedy. Point out that there have been some high points. Help illustrate that survivor's path.

Here are a few ideas. Balance out a visit to the grave site with a nice family dinner out. This speaks to your need to both remember and move forward. Have a special picture of your new family framed for your child as a tangible example of your stability as a unit and your commitment to each other.

Pick an event that was important to your loved one. Did Dad have a favorite team? Maybe he made it a tradition to take the kids to games. You can bring them too. It's a great way to connect you all together. Did Mom love music?

How about letting your child go through the entertainment listings and choose a concert for you all to attend?

Also understand these events do not have to come on the anniversary of the death. You can pick another date on the calendar that marks a special milestone or memory. Norman combined Sarah Ann's birthday with the great accomplishment of finishing that first year of middle school and delivered a great surprise.

"The last really fun thing Sarah Ann did with her mother before she got sick was take a trip to Disney World. They were only able to stay a day, and didn't even get to do all that much, but it was a memorable trip. So to reward Sarah Ann . . . and also reward me . . . for making it through a full school year and maintaining our sanity, I surprised her in her birthday card with the classic Super Bowl line: We're going to Disney World!"

What an amazing idea this is! Norman was able, in a single trip, to honor Sarah Ann's mom and the time they had together, celebrate the end of the first year of a new school and a new era in their lives together, as well as another year of Sarah Ann's life, and create an incredible bonding experience and memories that will last a lifetime.

"It was the best time I've ever had with my daughter," he said. "We were able to remember her mom by going on some of the rides they went on together. And we were able to celebrate getting through that year, which had definitely been a struggle."

There are so many lessons in this story. But the biggest

one is to realize that, as hard as things have been, there is still much to celebrate. Grief, for all its pain, also brings accomplishments. And these accomplishments provide the foundation for the strength that will get you and your children through the tough times ahead.

I once had lunch with a Kate's Club volunteer whose husband had passed away, leaving her with three children. She shared that they had just celebrated the tenth anniversary of his death. Her kids were now in college and had started families of their own. But for the past several years, the four of them had made it a point to have dinner or lunch together on the anniversary of her husband's death. This story shows that this ritual can be simple. It also shows us that it is something that can be carried on for years to come. After a certain amount of time you will have effectively transitioned the very reason you are getting together from a negative to a positive. Sure you will spend some of the day remembering and that may bring sadness. There is nothing wrong with that at all. But you will also give yourselves a chance to create a new tradition based on your all being together and celebrating not only the family you were, but the family you are.

The First Vacation

I don't recall what my family did that first anniversary of my mom's death. I do remember the first vacation that we took afterward and that was a hard transition to make. It was the first holiday season after my mom died (we'll talk more about handling holidays on page 145), and my dad decided that facing all those traditions and memories at home would be too hard. So we piled into the car and headed for Florida, where we would visit friends and relatives. The trip was a bonding moment for the three of us, though it closed the door on years of tradition—both for vacationing and the holidays. But my dad thought it was important that we charge ahead with new adventures; that has always been his approach to life. And he found it crucial to spend that time with family and friends, to remain connected and stabilized to a certain degree.

What I remember most about that week was the way the three of us came together. Nothing bonds people quite like adventure, and given all we had been through that year, this trip definitely qualified as that. We had spent months off on our own journeys, trying to find our respective ways through brand-new lives. The trip gave us a chance to strip all that away and be together. It was different from our trips in the past, but it provided a feeling of safety like almost nothing else had to that point. It confirmed for me, at least, that through it all, we were still a family.

Another mom once told me about her trepidation around this first trip as well. She came into my office after dropping her sons off one day and opened up about this fear, saying she had planned a family vacation, but just couldn't do it. I will tell you what I told her, which was that as hard as it might be to go on that trip, canceling it would deprive her family of joy that they richly deserved and desperately needed. It's all about getting back on that horse. The longer you put off reengaging in this treasured together time as a family, the more you risk further disconnects at home. In this mom's situation, to ease her completely understandable discomfort around this first trip, I encouraged her to have her kids and herself bring along friends. With this, she perked up and thought that was a great idea. Why? In the end, during these difficult times and transitions, I go back to my original plea that we are not meant to do this alone. She decided to bring a friend to support her. Her kids should reap the same benefits of this arrangement, even if their "support" came mostly in the form of play and fun with their friends.

A lot of your thoughts about this vacation are built around how you think about it beforehand. You have to understand that this will surely be a different trip than you are used to. You have to accept that there will be times during the trip that will bring sadness. Some you will expect and some you will never see coming. In the end, though, you are taking a really important step not only for yourself but for your family. You are blazing a trail for happiness and togetherness and creating a platform for a whole new set of memories that will sustain and define you in the years to come.

I have to say, as hard as this first vacation might be,

it will likely not be the hardest "first" you will face. I know from my own experience and from talking to all the kids and parents I am so fortunate to know, that the toughest first often arrives with the first hint of the holiday season.

Happy Holidays?

Nowadays, with the holiday marketing blitz hitting full throttle long before Thanksgiving dinner is served, the pressure of the holiday season on a grieving family is more magnified than ever. Family traditions are at the core of the holiday experience, and nobody willingly changes a good one. Everything can change, however, when we lose someone integral to that family unit.

For me, the holidays represented the biggest and most tangible changes to the childhood I had known before my mom's death. In our house, she was the one who rang every bell and hung every decoration possible for every holiday. She loved to celebrate them all. I am not sure my Dad knew what to do after she died. My mom and dad hosted a rather legendary annual Christmas Eve party (legendary in our family, anyway!), but that was just one of the tradition casualties that year. As I said, my family actually attempted to escape Christmas in our own house all together by hitting the road and traveling down south to visit family. Our home was still too haunting. No tree was put up that year, and the stockings, ones my mom had hand-stitched for all of us, were not hung. They just wouldn't be the same without her, and my father was preparing us for that in his own way.

His approach was to make the holiday a bit more exciting by being around family and ultimately ending up with friends at the beach. Warmer weather, he figured, was bound to certainly brighten the days. I think my dad made a smart choice. Though he wasn't building any new traditions that first year, he was showing us that old traditions were ending and that was OK. The first holidays are hard no matter how you slice it. Often I hear parents say that they are just trying to get through this time. Joy is seen as a luxury; they just want to make it to the end.

The best way to get through the season is to go into it acknowledging just how difficult it is going to be. I recommend taking a proactive approach by anticipating some of these difficulties. As the season approaches, take an inventory of your holiday traditions. What will have to change because this person is no longer there? What can be adjusted? How can you keep certain traditions alive? And what can be a new tradition that you start for the years to come? All of these are healthy measures that will make the impact of the holidays on your family just slightly more cushioned. And if you can't make all of this happen in the first year, that is completely OK. The first year will most likely be the hardest. In my family's case, the annual party did go on; it just took an extra year, and it began to happen at other locations. We always still had some celebration on that same evening for most years beyond my mother's death. It was different, but it was still satisfying. This is a good example of how traditions can still carry a footprint in your holiday season, but with some slight changes to them.

So how do you decide what to keep around and what to change? If you can, bring your children into this process. This is especially true for your older children. It brings you together, validates the things that they might be feeling and also helps you prepare as a family for the things that are to come. What you are doing here is integrating stability into change, and this is something your kids are bound to appreciate, if not this year, then in the years to follow.

Andi, a Kate's Club mom we introduced earlier, tells a story that is a great example of how to make this type of decision. "We tried to do things the way we had done them in the past," she said. "There were some special traditions in our house that we kept going. For instance, my husband had made what we called 'The Tacky Menorah' and we used it every year. It was six feet tall, made of heavy Styrofoam and painted blue. We decorated it as horribly as we possibly could and put our presents under it for fun."

Last year Andi noticed that this family staple was in great disrepair. "It was really starting to age and fall apart, and I got really upset about it. I said, 'OK, what are we gonna do here? Daddy made this and I don't know how to do it.' Then one of the boys said to me, 'It's blue. It's tacky. So go get yourself some painter's tape and just patch it up.' I laughed, and I did it!"

Andi's solution is a great example of what I always tell parents about family traditions. Work to find the right equilibrium between old and new. The other thing I love about the story is the way she involved her kids in the decision. Because they were brought into the conversation, the whole family was able to come to a resolution that they all could feel good about.

Another Kate's Club mom, Selvy, employed a different approach. Her husband's birthday fell just before Christmas, so she made it a point to do something special that first holiday season without him. She created a brand-new family tradition.

"Because of what we had learned at Kate's Club, we started taking an annual trip to Tybee Island. Josiah loved to do that sort of thing. So each year we go there and send balloons away in his memory. Sharing that experience somehow made things a little easier."

This family was fortunate in that they discovered this new healing tradition in the very first holiday season after Josiah died. You might not be as lucky. I can't stress enough how important it is to keep working at it. Your traditions may not appear as much as evolve. I urge you not to give up though. The rewards you will receive as they evolve are powerfully strong.

In fact, if you want to jump-start this discovery process,

sit down with your kids and talk about new traditions. Let each person talk about what traditions meant the most to him or her, and then share ideas on what new traditions might look or feel like. Learn from Andi's example of how she and her family created a new tradition that was both a continuation and a reinvention of a tradition they'd had before.

This is also a great time to continue family traditions by passing them down to the next generation. Let's say Dad was always the one who took the kids out to find that perfect holiday tree, or that decorating the mantel was Mom's job and hers alone. You can really empower your kids by passing jobs like this onto them. Sitting down with your kids and telling them that these types of traditions now belong to them is a powerful way to connect them to their loved one and also have them own a cherished family rite.

Helping Yourselves by Helping Others During the Holidays

I've found that a great strategy for grieving families facing the holidays is to turn the focus away from themselves by engaging in community service activities. This is something we do often with our Kate's Club kids. And you'd be amazed at how it opens up their eyes to the fact that there are others out there who are suffering and need help too. The act gives them valuable perspective while making them feel great about helping out. Why not make it a new tradition that you and your kids spend one Saturday (or as many as you can spare) during the holidays at a local soup kitchen or shelter? Is there a local toy drive in your community? How about organizing a "Secret Santa" effort for a local community agency? What a great way to show your kids that while what has happened to them is indeed tragic, there are things in their life for which they must be thankful, and there are others who are in even more desperate need. Helping others during times of need is one of the most empowering activities for grieving children and adults.

Most of all, remember this: Your loved one's death should never mean that the joy and meaning of the holiday season has to die as well. The season will bring forth memories forever, and those memories will be particularly powerful in those first years. Yet you can't lose sight of the fact that you must not live to grieve. You must live to *live* . . . and this is a great time to set your family on that healing path.

BOTH TRADITIONS AND TRANSITIONS ARE TIMES IN OUR lives when our characters are finely tuned. They are moments that build us to be who we are on just an average day. Your child is just starting to shape his character, and such events as the ones we have discussed in this chapter will be some of his most defining moments. Tread cautiously when supporting your child during these transitions, and do so with communication and love. It is some of the most important and lasting work you will do in setting the stage for her to be a survivor and not a victim—and a crucial building block for the foundation of your healing place.

CHAPTER EIGHT

Introducing a New Partner and Remarriage

Just when you might have thought your healing place was settling into being just that, one of the most profound changes and challenges can shake its very foundation. We covered many transition triggers in the last chapter. This one, however, I thought deserved its very own chapter: dating and remarriage.

This is one transition that has the potential to drive lasting wedges into the family structure. It is certain to be a time that will require extra care and attention to your children's life and their grief related to losing Mom or Dad.

It brings us back full circle to taking care of yourself. And specifically back to a healthy enough place in your life where you are ready to seek out an intimate, mature relationship. This is going to be sensitive terrain almost any way you handle it, given the rawness of the issues surrounding these life changes. I am not going to tell you how you should handle this situation for yourself. Rather, I want to help you learn how to best handle this situation with your kids.

I also have to tell you that this is the hardest chapter for me to write, for two reasons. First, I write this as someone who has never been on your side of the issue. I have never been a grieving widow or widower, and I have never been in your situation of rightfully seeking out the happiness you deserve while balancing the evolving needs of a still-grieving family. My experience here is from your child's side of the fence.

The second reason is that my particular experience with this topic was difficult and painful. My dad remarried two years after my mother's death, and it was without a doubt the hardest leg of my entire grief journey. From where I sit now it is easy to look back on the situation and see the kinds of mistakes that were made and the lasting impact they had. It is also easy to see that while my grief was heightened by this experience and my personal struggles extended by the way it was handled, my dad's intentions and need for this person to be in his life as well as in mine and my brother's were genuine.

I am going to key in on two tips that are simple but will have a lasting effect on how this transition unfolds in your home:

1. Communication is again key, and that communication must come from you.

2. This choice is yours, not your child's, so find ways your child can feel included in the process of this new person joining your family.

However, what you must know is that no matter how carefully and sensitively you might introduce this new person and new reality into your children's lives, you should be prepared for plenty of turbulence ahead. It is, after all, to be expected when you look at all you and your kids have been through.

Please don't think for a second that my sharing these potential difficulties is an attempt to dissuade you from taking this step. Remember that one of my core principles is the need for you to take care of yourself in order to take care of your children. I'm merely telling you to be prepared. And as we have talked about plenty of times so far in this book, the number one key to preparation is communication.

Before we talk about how to communicate with your children on this important topic, let's talk about you. This is a conversation I have had dozens of times, with parents in all kinds of situations. In every one of these conversations, even with all of these variables, there has been one constant: the parents almost always express that they feel significant guilt, whether it is related to their lost spouse, to their family, or more often, to both.

The reality is that it is perfectly normal for you to feel the need to bring a romantic relationship back into your life. It is a sign of your growth, a step on your journey and a cause for celebration as opposed to regret. As hard as it is to reconcile, you have to realize that being ready for this new phase in your life does nothing to diminish the love you had for your spouse.

But dipping your toe back in the relationship pool is not going to be easy. We all feel vulnerable putting ourselves back "out there." At the same time, however, this effort should also bring you a sense of empowerment that you are entitled to feel. So if you are ready to put yourself back out there, I say go for it! You totally deserve the excitement, happiness and comfort it can bring.

Do you feel a "but" coming on? You're right. Here come the disclaimers.

As an adult who had this experience of remarriage and a stepmother when I was a child, I look back at my dad's journey and completely understand why he needed this relationship in his life. At the time, though, I neither understood nor accepted his decision. It all goes back to what we talked about in Chapter 2. You need to reach down to your child and deal with her on her emotional level, not yours. Understand the limitations she has in trying to truly understand your needs, even if it seems that grief has allowed her a greater emotional understanding than she had before.

Getting It Right

A new marriage, or even a new relationship when your children are still living at home, may be the single most impactful event in your family's life since the death of your loved one.

Like I said, it all comes down to communication. And it all comes down to you.

You are in charge of how this relationship is introduced to your family and the role it will play for all of you. This is a lot of responsibility on your shoulders, but it is among the most important jobs you will do as the leader of your new family unit.

As you certainly know by now, each child's reaction is going to vary according to his or her age and ability to understand what is happening in your lives. The younger the child, the more you need to be sensitive to his or her concerns. It's difficult for young children to understand why you need or want this relationship, and you can't expect them to do so.

I strongly suggest that you do whatever you can to give your children comfort around this new situation. That might mean spending some extra dedicated time with them. Or it could mean just making the most of the time you do spend with them. Your goal here is to drive home the fact that this new person is not going to change the way you feel about your children. Remember that just like when his mom or dad died, your child is going to be extra sensitive to any changes in your relationship with him brought on by any new environment, situation or person.

The more gradually this new person enters your life (and subsequently your child's life), the more comfortable your child will feel. One way to accomplish this is to introduce the relationship in stages. For instance, if your new companion is suddenly around at all times, your child will recognize the change and likely react unfavorably to it.

I am not at all trying to diminish the importance of time with your new companion. I am just trying to share with you that this is a time when your child needs extra attention and affirmation. If this means you have to sacrifice some time in your new relationship, it is well worth the long-term benefits you will reap in your relationship with your family.

Now, the older the child gets, the more complicated this becomes. Why? Well, doesn't everything get a little more complicated with age? Your older children will be able to understand and assess this process much more. They will be carefully observing you and how you are handling the relationship and its effect on your family responsibilities.

I am a good example of this. I was then fourteen, so for me it was all about wondering why, suddenly, I was not enough for my dad. Having lost my mom, my fear of losing my dad as well had elevated him to a new position of importance and priority in my life. This went both ways. Not only was I concerned about how important he was to me, I was concerned about how important I was to him. His time and attention became my total validation as a young person. When that changed drastically due to a new relationship in his life, my self-esteem took a serious hit and insecurities developed.

I understood more and more over time why this relationship was important in his life, but it has taken many years for me to cope with this fracture in my self-esteem. If communication in my home had been more open, I think a lot of these growing insecurities could have been avoided. I also found that as it progressed, most of the communication about this relationship came not from my father, but from his new significant other.

Debrah's son Julian was eight years old when his dad died. When Debrah introduced the man she was seriously dating to the family, Julian saw him as a male threatening his relationship with his mom and his sisters. He saw it as a threat to his new role as man of the house, a role that had given him honor and helped him cope with his loss and new family structure.

It's understandable that a child like Julian would struggle with any man who entered his mom's life and subsequently took this role from him. It had nothing to do with who the man was. It had to do with any new man in his mom's life and any new man in his life. Debrah understood and acknowledged this dynamic. She took the mature route to accept the discomfort and put time and communication into nurturing this relationship between her new companion and Julian. Again, she took the two keys to this situation and used them. The communication and conversation about this new person needs to come from you, and you need to properly acknowledge how your decision to bring this person into your life also affects your children's lives.

Your New Relationship and Your Family: From Introduction to Integration

I don't envy any parent tiptoeing the sensitive lines of introducing a new person into a family affected by grief. However, I would give one bit of strong advice based on having been the child in such a situation myself. Remember that while you're starting a life with a new partner, you must never lose sight of the past life that made you a family. Integrating a new relationship into your family is just that: integration. It's not substitution or restarting. Make sure your new companion understands that.

When Debrah felt ready to enter another marriage, she was incredibly clear with her new husband about the ways in which she would continue to celebrate her former life and love. She continued to spend her wedding anniversaries at a table for one. She continued to spend time at the cemetery. She continued to attend her support group. It was all part of who she was and how she healed, and a credit to her partner's understanding of and respect for the situation.

Debrah is also quick to share that her kids did not exactly welcome this new man into their family right away. "I think they felt like I was going to forget their dad. They struggled with that." Her children's reactions provide good examples of how children's ages play an important role. "My oldest, Chanel, was upset. Very upset. She said 'He's not gonna tell me what to do. He's not my dad.' I explained to her that he was not trying to be her dad. That's not his role. Once I talked her through that and told her that just because I was remarrying didn't mean I was trying to replace her dad, she was OK."

This is a great example of how going that extra mile with your children, meeting them on their terms, can help the whole family. Debrah directly addressed her daughter's greatest fear and in the process helped smooth the path for her and her family's new life.

We talked about how Julian was worried that his new role in the family would change. Debrah also shared that when her new relationship became serious, she had addressed Julian's concerns by telling him she would wait to marry. When the engagement was announced, Julian had a particularly hard time with it. "It was nine months," Debrah said. "I told Julian that if I had to wait for him to give his blessings, I'd be an old lady!"

Here too is a great lesson. Answer your kids' concerns directly and you'll be amazed at the progress you can make and understanding you can earn.

Debrah was most surprised by the reaction of her middle child, Chloe. Chloe had been incredibly close to her Dad. Yet in the time since his passing, she had seen almost more than anyone the impact his loss had had on Debrah. "I remember on Valentine's Day she wrote a card to my significant other that said, 'Thanks for making my mom so happy.' She had seen me crying every day. She, almost more than anyone, knew how devastating the impact was on me. It is like through that death she and I have become closer than we ever were before." Grief can have all kinds of unexpected impacts on your kids' emotional development. As I have said, one of these impacts is that it can make them more compassionate and understanding. Chloe's reaction here is a wonderful example of that.

As you go through this process, keep in mind that it is completely because of a choice *you* made. That is not a negative, mind you. What I mean is that you have introduced into a grieving child's life another element that is beyond her control. Grieving children often crave control because death has taken so much of it from them already. They had no say in the matter. So in these scenarios, they often want to feel like they have some.

My advice is to do what Debrah did. Give them that feeling of control by being open and honest, by soliciting their opinions and stating yours. This is not to say their wants and needs will trump yours. You're the parent here. Empower your kids by saying, "You can decide the role you want this person to play in your life." It's about giving back some of that control. And, again, about communication. By putting these topics on the table, you are bringing your kids into the process and showing them that you value their input.

A big factor in this success story was the way Debrah's new partner handled the whole situation. Doing this the right way takes a unique understanding from your new partner, who needs to be able to anticipate and handle the resistance he or she will get from your kids. And to understand that turning this into a battle will do absolutely no good for anyone involved.

Here's another place where the onus of communication falls on you. You need to be open in sharing the details of your family dynamic with your partner. Help him or her get a full picture of the people involved, including your late spouse. The more information that person is armed with, the better chance he or she will have to enter and navigate the situation with the sensitivity it demands.

I have heard many stories of families who have gotten through this transition, and children who adore their stepparent. It doesn't always have to be the Cinderella disaster. I am so relieved when I hear peers of mine share great stories of remarriage after their mom or dad died when they were a child. There are several variables that set the stage for how a new relationship will impact your family unit. But if you have read this chapter for a reason and are most curious for direct practical advice, here are some key points to remember:

- Remain confident in your decision to date again— acknowledge the discomfort and guilt and grief it may bring up for you, but don't let it keep you from exploring this type of relationship in your life again.

- Remember these feelings that came up for you when you decided to integrate a new relationship, a new person, into your child's life. While you had control of that decision for yourself, your child doesn't have that control, so be sensitive to his adverse reaction to anyone new in Mom or Dad's life. And now in their lives as well . . .

- Communicate. You should communicate with your children about every step that the relationship progresses to. Answer their questions and address their needs. Make sure that communication is coming from you.

- Communicate with your new partner. He or she needs to be just as prepared for and understanding about your family's past and your children's evolving life with grief as a part of it.

So while my personal experience was not ideal, I've heard many more success stories than failures in this arena. I am confident that if you approach this transition in your child's life with the care and honesty it needs, it will be a succcess for your family as well. To see you in a happy, healthy relationship again will bring joy into your child's life as well. That may not happen right at the beginning, but it will come. And when it does, it will also restore their confidence that, in relationships, endings are new beginnings, and they have many more to come in their young lives.

CHAPTER NINE

Maintaining Your Healing Place:
What's Life and What's Grief

So we've come to our last chapter together. It was never my intention to cover every aspect of a family's grief journey. In fact I think that type of book would need as many volumes as an encyclopedia and would still be woefully incomplete. There is a reason for that. Life is uncertain to begin with, but when you add the experience of a lost loved one, that uncertainty is magnified beyond what you even knew was possible. At the beginning of this book I welcomed you to the club. At Kate's Club, when you join, you're a member for life. While we only serve school-aged children, we welcome you with the understanding that your grief and your child's grief is not transactional. There is no closing out of our grief. It is transformative. You and your family's lives have been forever changed by this death. Your goal and my goal is to make sure we make the best of that change.

We have talked about the fundamentals of creating a healing place in your home through this book. Now I want to leave you with some tips on maintaining grief amid life's uncertainties, while not letting it inhibit too much of you and your child's growth as healthy, happy individuals.

In the grief field it is common to read that grieving children often have more anxiety than those children who have not experienced a significant loss. Bereaved children have shown a tendency to externalize their control issues because they are more likely to feel that their fate is not in their hands and the uncertainties of life are overwhelming.

With this tendency in mind, your healing place should evolve into somewhere your child finds comforts in times of anxiety and ease alike. Because, as we've discussed, both of those times are bound to come.

To help you do this, I have put this chapter together as a sort of maintenance plan. I hope that by reading this book, you will find your journey made easier and your grief more manageable thanks to your new awareness and preparedness.

As you continue to love and support your family, remember three things:

- Your kid is still a kid—she will still have everyday kid struggles that may not be related to grief.

- Your kid is still a kid—allow him to seek out and enjoy

those experiences in childhood that all kids deserve to enjoy. Grief doesn't stop life.

- Your kid is still a kid—she needs to remain a priority in your life, which means you remain accessible and available to her for support. Your child's grief as a result of Mom or Dad dying will be an event that forever impacts him, but it doesn't define him.

You will continue to experience transitions, both changes that directly relate to the person who died and those that do not. Know that any transition in your child's life has the possibility to be a trigger of grief emotions.

But also remember that not all emotions or struggles are grief-related. Be careful to not put your child's life experiences all in this one box. We are all multidimensional, and your child has just begun to expand these dimensions in life. I'll explain more about this later in the chapter, with a great example of a teenage girl who struggled through being selected for her high school's homecoming court.

First, however, I want to take a quick moment and give you some perspective on how to look at your family moving forward. Remember it's not about getting over your loved one's death, but it is about moving forward. Your life today, the people you have become and the people who surround and support you are your "new normal."

Seeking a "Normal" Life Together

"Normal." Now there's a tough word to quantify when it comes to grief. In talking with grieving kids and their parents, I am often asked if things will ever return to "normal." Talk about your loaded question.

There is no such thing as normal when it comes to kids and grief. A fundamental change in life ultimately settles back into something, but that something is anything but normal.

A child I talked to not long after her dad passed away was the one who called this phase her "new normal." I thought it was a great way of looking at things. She was acknowledging that she was on a path toward healing, yet nothing in her life would ever be exactly the same as it once was. As much as kids crave a return to their normal life and normal routines, it would be misleading and disingenuous of us even to use the word. The "new normal" approach, however, shows an understanding that the path is now different, but it is a path that may ultimately deliver comfort, happiness and stability for the child as an individual and for the family as a whole.

It is likely that, at some point, your child will bring up the idea of "normalcy." I encourage you to engage her in this conversation and to let her know that she holds a tremendous amount of power in determining just what "normal" will mean in her life. This can be incredibly empowering for a child who has had such a vital part of life taken away, a child who feels no sense of control over anything at all. When talking to kids who want everything to return to "normal"—I ask them what "normal" means. A very common response is "I just want to be comfortable." Kids seem to interchange these words. So focus on making life comfortable for your kids again as opposed to normal. Your healing place is what can bring them that comfort. All the things in this book that are the building blocks of that place—communication, memories, support, and so on—can bring that comfort to your home and family. It is when they discover comfort that your children will begin to truly adjust to this new normal.

Normalcy for kids can also be directly related to a routine. Once the storm quiets down in your home and you begin your quest to build your healing place, routine can play a key role in your success. Try and get back to the routines your kids are used to. If they were used to having dinner at a certain time, do what you can to return to that schedule. If they normally did homework right after dinner each evening, keep that schedule as well.

I realize the changes in your life may not always make this possible. But I urge you, as much as you can, to give your kids the chance to return to the routines that made them comfortable. In a world where everything is changing for them, there can be great comfort in returning to the patterns of their lives that are possible to re-create in your new life.

Kids today have more exposure to families not fitting the traditional mold of a mother and a father and siblings. There are so many dynamic family structures in today's world that kids focus less on the physical makeup of their family. But they do focus on dynamics, such as how their family functions and feels.

With this in mind, do all you can to keep your children a priority and to keep focusing on communication as a tool you can all use. Open communication is not always going to be easy. You know that by now. But you also likely know that open and honest communication can be the perfect antidote for anxiety and fear.

Paying Attention to Self-Esteem

A common challenge for grieving children is how this life event impacts their self-esteem. "Feeling different" is a core reason for this developmental adversity. Children's lives are about belonging and feeling accepted. A big fear I experienced, and that I have seen other kids experience, was the worry that I was now different from my peers. I encourage you to talk to your children about how our differences make us unique, how they make us who we are. No one else can determine who we are except ourselves.

Your child's desire for acceptance by his peers may keep him from acknowledging his grief. Help him see how his grief can make him a stronger, more special person. I wish

I could tell every grieving child that this experience, while tragic, also provides you with the opportunity to overcome adversity and to understand and spread compassion. This compassion comes from a new perspective of truly valuing what the world has to offer. Having been in these children's shoes and been through many storms of my own grief since my mom died, I have also had the beautiful and empowering experience of the rainbows that follow these storms. My adversity has brought me happiness and courage and compassion. Remember what I said about grief being love? It probably sounded strange at the time, but I hope you can see now what I meant.

I would love to spend one day with my mom, but I also wouldn't trade my life for anyone else's. I can't share this with your children, but you can. You can tell them about your own struggles through childhood and how they helped to build you to be the person you are today.

Focus on Life

Your maintenance plan also includes continuing to try to return your child's focus to life rather than death and grief. I want to share a story with you about one family who accomplished this in an inspiring way.

It came from a family with five children, ranging in age from infancy to teenagers. The father had passed away and left a mom to raise the children. Right after her husband died, she arranged to have a family photo done. For many families this is a huge hurdle for years to come. Many parents just can't bring themselves to continue traditions like this one, even if it means missing out on priceless keepsakes. It's just too hard.

This mom, however, had a plan. She told the children to dress themselves up however they wanted. She wanted them to don whatever clothes, uniform or costume they felt best captured who they were at that moment as individuals. She was taking a potentially devastating milestone, that first family picture, and turning it into an opportunity for these kids to express themselves in a living moment. Even more important, by doing this, she was making the incredibly important statement that in spite of their tragedy, they were and always would be a *family*.

The result of that session is a large print that hangs not only in Mom's home but in the home of each child. It carries with it a simple message: accept your grief, but don't let it keep you from focusing on life. This exercise also helps each child grab ahold of his or her individual identity. Chances are, it won't be that different from what it was before Mom or Dad died. A photo like this can serve as a reminder of that. Grieving children's families have changed. Their whole lives have changed. But they need to understand that despite all that, at the core of it all, they are still who they were and they will still be loved and cared for by those who surround them.

Grief Support Never Ends

Parents of grieving kids always worry about how these kids are doing. But as is typical of our culture, they can also get caught up in the notion that this "recovery" is something that happens in the time immediately following a loss. The truth is the ramifications of loss on a child's life continue to reveal themselves in large and small ways for many years, and in lots of cases forever.

It was the spring of my junior year of high school. I had my sights set on a prom date who was actually one of my best friends. I just knew that the prom would provide him with the perfect opportunity to change gears and accept what had been so obvious all year long.

So one afternoon, I was at a girlfriend's house with a few other friends and she sat me down to let me know that this boy had in fact asked *her* to the prom. She knew I would have some sensitivity around this and just wanted to clear it with me. I was completely blindsided. However, if I had learned one thing in the four years since my mom's death, it was how to mask even the rawest of emotions. Remember, I didn't have a healing place, so I didn't have a safe place to put such emotions. I just had myself. So I smiled and told her it was fine, even that I was excited for her and really wanted her to go. Then I resolved to get the heck out of that house as fast as humanly possible. I got as far as my car before I completely lost it. I'm not sure I had ever felt so alone and so unsure of where I should go next.

Where I went showed more than anything how lost I was. Within minutes I was sitting on a hillside, at my mother's grave, spilling more tears than I thought I had in me.

At the time I went to my mother's grave as a way to find comfort and a safe place to let my emotions out. I'm certainly glad I did. But to truly have a healing place, you need people to be a part of it. Even though this particular life experience could have happened to me without grief as a part of my life, my emotions were compounded because I was looking for the comfort of my mother and she was no longer there. You may not be able to catch every fall your child takes in life, but she should know that you are always accessible to help her get back up.

Teens Will Be Teens: Not All Behavior Is Grief-Related

One of my favorite movie scenes comes from the film *Love Actually.* In the scene, a father who is a new widower is talking to his stepson, the stepson he will now be raising alone. The scenes leading up to this one make it clear that these two are truly paralyzed in their grief. The young boy doesn't speak much to his stepfather, or, for that matter, to anyone else. For his part, the stepfather is deeply saddened and concerned, but has no idea what to do. After airing his worries to a close friend, he decides it is best to confront the boy.

The two are sitting on a bench in London. It's a trademark dreary London day and they are completely silent. Finally gaining the courage to find out what is wrong, the father asks his stepson, "What is the problem, Samuel? Is it just Mom?"

The boy looks at him, pauses and says, "Well, truth is, actually, I'm in love." He goes on to say, "I know I should be thinking about Mom all the time, and I am, but the truth is, I'm in love."

The scene illustrates a key point for all parents. Just because your child has gone through the pain of loss does not mean that he is not going to experience those typical things that every child, grieving or not, is going to go through.

The look on the stepdad's face says it all. There is almost a sense of relief that the issue is not grief-related. The look signals the realization that yes, he has a young boy who has been impacted by grief, but he also has a young boy who is going to experience all the typical confusing and wonderful issues this stage of life brings with it—in this case, the total exhilaration of a first crush!

This is a great example that it is perfectly OK for you and your child to be on different emotional pages. However, instead of continuing to worry about it, the stepdad in this case was brave enough to ask the question. It's a great scene and, I am quite sure, represents a pretty common scenario in the lives of grieving families.

There is no way to look at your child and know "Is it

grief or is it life?" Yet I always advise parents who ask me this question to go ahead and ask it directly to their child. Here's another great tip this scene brings up. Throw away timetables. The stepfather's first response to the boy is, with a chuckle, "Well, aren't you a little young to be in love?"

The truth is that based on the mature experiences your child has experienced around loss, it is more than likely that she is more in tune with emotions and may be more emotionally advanced than a peer might be. It is important that you acknowledge this fact as you move forward together.

"Courting" Trouble: Allison's Story

Allison was a teenager at Kate's Club who kind of reminded me of myself at that age. She was incredibly active, very involved with friends and activities and academics. One day her mom came to me very worried because Allison didn't want to go to school. The new phase had kind of crept up on her, her mother said, and by the time she even noticed it, Allison was pretty far along in her funk.

Her mom assumed the issues surrounded Allison's loss. My immediate thought was that it was Allison's first year of high school. Such transitions are classic traps for kids in her situation . . . new place, new people, new teachers, new friends . . . all potential triggers for grief-related anxiety.

So I decided to talk to Allison during a Kate's Club outing—I remember it was at a museum—and see if I could learn some more about what was going on. We were just sort of casually moving through the exhibit hall and I asked her how school was going.

The answer was a quick "Fine." I knew she had been looking forward to cheerleading and I asked how that was going. "Fine" came even quicker. I tried asking about how the team was doing. Same answer. I was getting nowhere. I returned to the cheerleading topic, thinking I might have seen a little opening there. She had made varsity as a freshman, and I thought maybe giving her a chance to share about something she was proud of might get us somewhere. I told her that was quite an accomplishment. "Yeah," she said, "but it's hard."

After opening a little bit more about her fears around her cheerleading, we came upon the topic of homecoming. OK, now we were on to something big. Boys! That could keep any young girl from wanting to go to school.

The problem wasn't boys. The problem was that Allison had been chosen to be on the homecoming court. Here was a testament to her popularity with her peers, to her beauty and to her character. Who would ever be upset with that?

"Allison," I said, "that is so awesome! You should be thrilled. When is the game? I want to come and watch you walk out onto the field!"

"No you won't," she answered. "I'm not going to walk. Dads walk their daughters down the field, and I don't have a dad."

Bingo. Allison did not feel comfortable sharing this with her mom, because her mom had her own grief to deal with in addition to the added pressures of raising a family on her own. Allison believed this was her burden to bear, and she was making the choice not to bear it at all, to walk away from the situation in an attempt to make it go away.

The problem was that in doing so she was depriving herself of an incredibly positive event and an important honor. She was making the choice to let the weeds win out over the flowers, mainly because she did not have the support to face the issue head-on. I became that support just by engaging her in that conversation and facilitating her admission, perhaps for the first time even to herself, that this was the real issue here. Notice it didn't come right out. Be patient with conversation and communication, especially with teens. And for those of you with teens, I know I don't need to tell *you* that! As we chatted more, I was able to reason with Allison that certainly another male figure could walk her down the field. Who would that be? An uncle? A family friend? Heck, I even suggested us finding a buddy who could do it. She giggled at that one. But together we came away understanding that the show could go on and that she could be excited about the game and the dance and the experience even though her dad had passed away. All it took was asking a few of the right questions and working with her to make things clear, and she was back in the flowers again.

I am sure you never imagined your life would include the kind of balancing acts you now have to perform on a daily basis. How can you possibly help your children come to terms with profound loss while urging them to move forward with life? As with so many of the issues we have covered, the answer lies in communication. And the older your child gets, the more complex those communication issues can become.

You must never lose sight of the role you play in all of this. As I've said before, you are the primary architect of your child's healing place. You have the most influence when it comes to shaping your family's new normal. You are the guardian of innocence who can make sure that your kid, through it all, gets to still be a kid.

And maybe most important, you are the one who can both tell and show your kids that while their lives have changed, there is so much hope ahead. And we all know by now that it is this hope that powers every grieving journey and that has the ability to fill young lives with the happiness they deserve.

Don't Look for Closure to Grief, Look for Life's New Opportunities

"Closure" is an interesting word when it comes to grief. I think we have funerals to bring closure to a life. But as we have gone over, grief is more about mourning a relationship than it is about physical loss. The idea of closure, when it comes to relationships, is far different.

If we are honest, we will admit to ourselves that there is no end to grief, no checklist to get through. I know in our culture that is a hard pill to swallow. But if you face grief with this expectation rather than an expectation that it will end, I promise a more peaceful journey. It's one of the best examples you, as the adult in the household, can set for your children.

Yet still, the face of grief is always changing. But for all the variances that come into each life after a loved one passes away, one thing runs through them all: you aren't alone. Life is about relationships—we win some and we lose some. But we should always strive to surround ourselves with the people who are best equipped to help us support ourselves and our children.

Every time I walk into our clubhouse, I am greeted by a bunch of kids who display remarkable amounts of sympathy, compassion, tolerance and strength. They inspire me to display these same qualities.

In the same way, your child can inspire you. You and your child have so much to live for. And believe me I know that there are so many times it just feels wrong not to have that special person along for the ride.

Your children look to you for guidance and hope, even when you don't think they are paying attention. Love them more for their grief, and support them more in their lives. Life is about change, and we truly define ourselves in times of change. Helping your children define themselves in a healthy manner after this experience will without a doubt put them on a course to become the people they want to be—and a stronger version of it.

We use the commitment, energy and expertise of our staff and volunteers to hold up the healing walls of Kate's Club. We are thankful for an ever-evolving array of programs and exercises that give our kids a unique brand of support and enrichment. I hope that you can use some of what you have learned in this book to shore up your own healing walls. Because, as I have said, the foundation you provide your child with there will largely determine the success of his or her grief journey . . . and yours. As I've said, I sure wish I could give you a prescription for success. That is ultimately for you to find, and I hope the tools I have provided will help guide your way.

I am honored and heartened that you have chosen to allow me to share your journey. I wish you the healthiest and, yes, happiest of journeys. Here's to our meeting again somewhere along the path to most hope.

From my healing place to yours . . .

Kate

As I mention throughout the book, neither you nor your child should ever have to feel that you are alone. Outside of the healing support you all are providing for each other inside your home, there are many resources throughout the country that can also help you and your children learn to cope with your loss in a healthy and empowering way. Here is a state-by-state list of some of these resources.

ALABAMA

Huntsville
The Caring House
256-650-1212

Tuscumbia
The Healing Place
256-383-7133

ALASKA

Eagle River
TAPS: Tragedy
   Assistance Program
   for Survivors
800-959-TAPS

ARIZONA

Scottsdale
New Song Center for Grieving
   Children
480-951-8985

Tucson
Children to Children
520-322-9155

ARKANSAS

Little Rock
Kaleidoscope Kids
501-666-9697 x231
www.kaleidoscopekids.org

CALIFORNIA

Camarillo
Camarillo Hospice
805-389-5898

Claremont
Children/Family Bereavement
    Support
909-399-3289

Concord
Comfort for Kids
800-400-2820

Eureka
Hospice of Humboldt
707-444-8616

Los Angeles
Our House
310-475-0299
www.ourhouse-grief.org

Marin County
Hospice of Marin Children's
    Program
415-927-2273

Monterey
Community Hospital
    of Monterey
831-642-9269

Monterey
Griefbuster
831-649-1772

Palm Desert
The Mourning Star Center
760-836-0360
www.mourningstar.org

Palo Alto
Kara
650-321-5272
www.kara-grief.org

Petaluma
Hospice of Petaluma
707-778-6242

Redding
Mercy Hospice
530-224-1386

San Diego
Hospice of Grossmont Hospital
619-293-3337

San Diego
Rainbow Kids Bereavement
    Program
619-667-1900

San Diego
San Diego Hospice
619-688-1600 x529

Santa Clara
Healing Heart Program
408-980-9801

Santa Rosa
Memorial Hospice
707-568-1094

Sebastopol
VNA, Home Hospice
707-823-2419

Yreka
Madrone Hospice
530-842-3160

COLORADO

Boulder
Kid's Grief Group
303-415-3410

Denver
Judi's House
720-941-0331
www.judishouse.org

Evergreen
Camp Comfort, Mt. Evans
  Hospice
303-674-6400

Fort Collins
Kids Grief Connection
970-663-3500

Grand Junction
Forget-Me-Not
970-241-3770

Greeley
Hospice & Palliative Care
  of North Colorado
970-352-8487

CONNECTICUT

Bridgeport (Fairfield Cty)
Children's Bereavement Support
  Group, Hospice at Home
203-366-3821

Colchester
Colchester Counseling
  Association
860-537-5280

Danbury
Bereavement Center for Children
  & Families, Regional Hospice
  of Western Connecticut
203-797-1685

Greenwich
The Den for Grieving Kids
203-869-4848
www.familycenters.org

Hartford
Sibling Bereavement Support
  Group for Children,
  Connecticut Children's
  Medical Center
860-545-9879
www.ccmckids.org

New Milford
Children's Bereavement
  Programs, New Milford VNA
  Hospice
860-354-2216

Wallingford
Teen Grief Support Group,
    Connecticut VNA Hospice &
    Palliative Care
203-679-5300

Watertown
Camp Jonathon
860-274-5367

Windsor
Mary's Place, A Center for
    Grieving Children & Families
860-688-9621

DELAWARE

Statewide
New Hope
302-479-2577 x134

DISTRICT OF COLUMBIA

District
Wendt Center for Loss & Healing
202-624-0010

FLORIDA

Daytona Beach
Begin Again Children's Grief
    Center
904-258-5100

Fort Myers
Hope Hospice
941-489-9156
www.hopehospice.org

Lakeland
Bethany Center
863-687-1669

Maitland
New Hope Center for Grieving
    Children
407-599-0909

Miami
Children's Bereavement Center
305-668-4902
www.childbereavement.org

Naples
Children's Grief Workshops
941-261-4404

Orlando
Horizons Children's Loss
    Program
407-682-0808

Riviera Beach
Hearts & Hands Project
561-882-3100

Stuart
Children's Program, Hospice
    of Martin & St. Lucie
561-287-7860

Tallahassee
Children's Program, Big Bend
  Hospice
850-878-5310

Tavares
Children's Program, Hospice
  of Lake & Sumter
352-742-6808

West Melbourne
Bright Star Center for Grieving
  Children
321-733-7672

West Palm Beach
Hearts & Hope
561-832-1913

GEORGIA

Atlanta
Kate's Club
404-347-7619
www.katesclub.org

Marietta
Rising Sun Center for Loss &
  Renewal
770-928-1027

Milledgeville
Hospice of the Oconee
912-453-8572

Savannah
Kids Group & Kids Camp,
  Hospice Savannah
912-355-2289

IDAHO

Boise
Camp Erin (Life's Doors
  Hospice)
208-275-0000
www.lifesdoors.com/camperin.htm

Statewide
Touchstone
208-377-3216
www.touchstonecenter.org

Lewiston
Willow Center
208-746-6898

ILLINOIS

Arlington Heights
Willow House
847-940-0779
www.willowhouse.org

Belleville
KidsTime
618-234-2120 x1091

Chicago
Center for Grief Recovery &
    Sibling Loss
773-274-4600

Chicago
The Children's Place
773-395-9193

Chicago
Heartlight
773-880-4309

Geneva
Free to Be/Courage Quest,
    Fox Valley Hospice
630-232-2233

Glenview
Midwest Palliative & Hospice
    Care Center
800-331-5484
www.carecenter.org

Gurnee
Willow House
847-940-0779

Joliet
Family Journey
815-740-4104

Matteson
Vitas Hospice, Children's
    Bereavement
708-748-8777

Ottawa
Treasure of Life
815-434-4409

Palos Park
Healing Heart Program, Centre
    for New Beginnings
708-923-1116

Park Ridge
Good Mourning
847-699-2000

Rolling Meadows
Rainbows
847-952-1770
www.rainbows.org

Western Spring
Buddy's Place
708-354-0826
www.pillarscommunity.org/
    programs/BuddysPlace.asp

INDIANA

Fort Wayne
Erin's House for Grieving
    Children
219-423-2466
www.erinshouse.org

Indianapolis
Brooke's Place for Grieving
    Young People
317-879-4066

New Albany
Hospice of Southern Indiana
812-945-4596

Richmond
Mending Hearts
765-983-3101 x2932

South Bend
Camp Evergreen, Hospice
of St. Joseph County
219-243-3100

IOWA

Des Moines
Amanda the Panda
515-223-4847
www.amandathepanda.org

Des Moines
Healing Hearts
515-243-5221

Des Moines
Little Hands at Hamilton's
515-243-5221

Des Moines
Hospice of Central Iowa
515-274-3400

Lake City
HUGS Children's Support
Group
712-464-3171

Oskaloosa
Hospice of Mahaska County
515-672-3260

KANSAS

Hutchinson
Kids Kamp, Hospice of Reno
County
316-665-2473

Overland Park
Kids' Connection
816-333-1980

Wichita
Three Trees
316-683-2081

KENTUCKY

Berea
Renew: Center for Personal
Recovery
606-986-7878
www.renew.net

Erlanger
Stars: Grief Support for Kids
859-292-0244
www.starsforchildren.com

Henderson
St. Anthony's Hospice
502-826-2326

Lexington
Daniel's Care, Hospice of the
    Bluegrass
606-276-5344

Louisville
The Center for Grief & Loss
    at Hospice of Louisville
502-459-2100 x195

Louisville
Drawbridges
502-454-7564

LOUISIANA

Baton Rouge
Children's Bereavement Group
225-924-1431

MAINE

Brunswick
Transitions: Living Through Loss
    & Grief
207-721-9702

Kittery Point
Grief Support Center for
    Children & Families
207-439-5071

Lewiston
A Program for Grieving Children
    & Teens
207-777-8520

Portland
Center for Grieving Children
207-775-5216

Waterville
Camp Ray of Hope
207-873-3615

York
Grief Support Center for
    Children & Families
207-363-9151

MARYLAND

Chestertown
Camp Sunrise: A Family
    Bereavement Program
410-778-7058

LaPlata
Promises
301-934-1268

Millerville
Kidscene
410-987-2129

Queenstown
Camp New Dawn: Hospice
    of Queen Anne's
410-827-0426

Towson
Me Too! Program
410-252-4500 x287

MASSACHUSETTS

Arlington
The Children's Room
781-641-4741

Boston
The Circle
617-414-4005

Danvers
Children & Teens Bereavement
  Support Groups
978-774-7566

Fairhaven
Hospice of Community
  Nurse
508-999-3400

Hingham
The Circle
617-414-4005

Northampton
The Garden
413-584-3796
www.garden-cgc.org

Pittsfield
Hospice Care in Berkshires
413-443-2994

Plymouth
Children's Bereavement
  Program
508-830-2720

Various Towns
Family Loss Project/Network
800-814-9100

MICHIGAN

Adrian
Hospice of Lenawee
517-263-2323

Detroit
Sand Castles Grief Support
313-874-6881

Holland
Kids Grieve Too, Hospice
  of Holland
616-396-2972

Jackson
Grief & Growth
517-769-4853

Lansing
Ele's Place
517-482-1315

Livonia
Growing Through Grief
734-464-7810

Owosso
Memorial Healthcare Center
  Children's Bereavement
  Group
517-725-2299

Sault Ste. Marie
Good Grief Group, Hospice
 of Chippewa Cty
906-632-2202

St. Joseph
Lory's Place
269-983-2707

Westland
Connections
734-522-4244

MINNESOTA

St. Paul
HealthEast Hospice
651-232-3665

MISSOURI

Kansas City
Solace House
913-341-0318
www.solacehouse.org

St. Louis
Family Center for Grief
 Support
314-996-5105

St. Louis
The Kids' Clubhouse
314-727-4664

St. Louis
St. Louis Bereavement Center
 for Young People
314-965-5015

MONTANA

Great Falls
My Mom's/Camp Francis
406-455-2820

NEBRASKA

Fremont
Rainbows & Camp Mend a Heart
402-721-0817

Lincoln
Charlie Brown's Kids: Good
 Grief
402-483-1845

Omaha
Ted E. Bear Hollow
402-502-2773
www.tedebearhollow.org

NEW HAMPSHIRE

Concord
Growing Through Grief
603-224-4093 x4845
www.crhc.org

Dover
Pete's Place
603-740-2689

Exeter
Bridges
603-778-7391

Keene
Good Mourning Children
603-352-7799

Nashua
Good Grief, Home Health &
  Hospice Care
603-882-2941

Rochester
GAPS
603-335-7777

NEW JERSEY

Statewide
New Jersey Self-Help
  Group Clearinghouse
973-989-1122 (NJ only)
800-367-6274
  (outside NJ)

Brick
Art Therapy at Medical
  Center of Ocean County
732-206-8340

Flemington
Hunterdon Hospice Youth
  Bereavement Program
908-788-6600

Linden
Center for Hope
908-486-0700

Medford
Samaritan Hospice Marlton
609-654-1118

Montclair
Comfort Zone Camp
973-364-1717
www.comfortzonecamp.org

Montclair
Rainbows New Jersey State
  Chapter
973-744-8282
www.rainbowsnj.org

Northfield
The Alcove Center for Grieving
  Children & Families
609-484-1133
www.thealcove.org

Vineland
Children Living with a Loss,
  Hospice Care of South
  Jersey
609-794-1515

NEW MEXICO

Albuquerque
New Mexico Grief Services
   Program
505-272-0729

Farmington
Camp Michael Retreat
505-327-3739

Las Cruces
Center for Grief Services,
   Mesilla Valley
505-523-4700

Taos
Golden Willow Retreat
575-776-2024
www.goldenwillowretreat.org

NEW YORK

Babylon
Good Samaritan Hospice
   Children's Bereavement
516-376-3850

Brooklyn
The Healing Center
718-780-1899

Brooklyn
Metropolitan Hospice of Greater
   New York
718-630-2649

Buffalo
Storm Clouds & Rainbows:
   Shelter from the Storm
716-836-6460
www.hospicebuffalo.org

Elmhurst
St. Adalbert Church
718-429-2005

Larchmont
The Sanctuary: A Resource
   Center for Grieving Children
   & Families
914-834-4906, 914-834-6763

New York
Heartbridge Center for Loss
212-865-6742

Oneonta
Children/Teen Grief Support
   Group, Catskill Area Hospice
607-432-6773

Rochester
Kids Adjusting Through Support
716-232-5287

Roslyn Heights
The Cottage
516-626-1971

Sleepy Hollow
Phelps Hospice
914-366-3325

Syracuse
The Center for Living with
    Loss
315-634-1100

Syracuse
Hope for Bereaved, Center
    for Grieving Children &
    Families
315-475-9675
www.hopeforbereaved.com

Tuckahoe
The Tree House
914-961-2818 x317

Uniondale
Mercy Hospice, Community
    Bereavement
516-485-3060

Westbury
Hospice Care Network
516-666-6863

NORTH CAROLINA

Asheville
Children in Grief, Mountain
    Area Hospice
828-255-0231

Charlotte
Kinder-Mourn
704-376-2580

Forest City
Rainbows Grief Support Group
828-245-0095

Pinehurst
Camp Lost & Found: When
    Someone You Love Dies
910-215-6000

Wilmington
The Sunrise Kids, Lower Cape
    Fear Hospice
910-772-5463

NORTH DAKOTA

Fargo
Kids & Teens Grieve Too
701-237-4629

OHIO

Akron
Children's Grief Group
330-762-2557

Ashtabula
Hospice Hugs
440-997-6619

Cincinnati
Hospice of Cincinnati,
    Expressions Program
513-792-6914

Resources

Cincinnati
Fernside: A Center for Grieving
  Children
513-841-1012
www.fernside.org

Cleveland
Michael's House
440-338-5936

Columbus
Mt. Carmel Hospice & Evergreen
  Center
614-234-0200

Columbus
Hospice at Riverside & Grant
614-566-5377

Delaware
The Hope Center
740-368-5223

Elyria
The Phoenix Center for Grieving
  Children
440-934-1482

Girard
Kids Grieve Too
330-539-9238

Liberty Township
Companions on a Journey
  Grief Support
513-870-9108
www.companionsonajourney.org

North Canton
Center for Grief Counseling &
  Education
330-497-2960

Steubenville
Valley Hospice
740-283-7487

Zanesville
Helping Us Grieve
  Successfully
740-454-5353

OKLAHOMA

Bartlesville
A Place of Hope
918-336-1510

Edmond
The Kids' Place
405-844-5437
www.kidsplace.org

Tulsa
The Tristesse Center
918-587-1200
tristessecenter@sbcglobal.net

OREGON

Bend
Hospice of Bend, LaPine
541-389-4455

Coos Bay
Light House Center
541-269-2986

Eugene
Courageous Kids
541-461-7550

Medford
Winter Spring Center for Living
    with Loss & Grief
541-772-2527

Portland
The Dougy Center & National
    Center for Grieving
    Children
503-775-5683
www.dougy.org

Portland
Kaiser Permanente Cancer
    Counseling Center
503-331-6553

Portland
Me Too & Company
503-499-5307

Portland
Stepping Stones
503-285-8308

Redmond
Hospice of Redmond &
    Sisters
541-548-7483

Salem
Mother Oaks Child
503-399-7141

Tillamook
Adventist Health &
    Hospice
503-842-2588

PENNSYLVANIA

Dillsburg
Camp Koala
717-606-9934
www.campkoala.org

Lionville
Mommy's Light
610-725-9790
www.mommyslight.org

Philadelphia
Evenstar Bereavement Program,
    Children's Hospital
    of Philadelphia
215-590-3273

Philadelphia
Family Home Hospice
888-467-9330 x2362

Philadelphia
Center for Grieving
    Children, Teens &
    Families
215-427-6767

Lancaster
Hospice of Lancaster County
717-391-2412
www.hospiceoflancaster.org

New Freedom/York
Hearts Can Heal
717-235-4451

Radnor
Peter's Place, Center for Grieving
    Children & Families
610-687-5150
www.petersplaceonline.org

Pittsburgh
The Caring Place
412-544-1689

RHODE ISLAND

Providence
Friends Way
401-921-0980
www.friendsway.org

SOUTH CAROLINA

Charleston
Hospice Health Services
843-852-2177

Columbia
Brett's Rainbow
803-296-3100
www.palmettohealth.org

SOUTH DAKOTA

Rapid City
Hospice of the Hills
605-341-0632

TENNESSEE

Chattanooga
The Mourning After
423-892-9772

Knoxville
Harbor Center for Grief &
    Family Transitions
423-947-0146

Knoxville
Children/Parent Bereavement
    Support Group, University of
    Tennessee Medical Center
423-544-9704

TEXAS

Amarillo
SKY-Crown of Texas Hospice
806-372-7696

Dallas
Healing Hearts, St. Paul Hospice
214-956-9441

El Paso
Children's Grief Center of El Paso
915-532-6004

Fort Worth
Camp El Tesoro de la Vida
817-831-2111

Fort Worth
The Warm Place
817-870-2272
www.thewarmplace.org

Houston
Camp Kaleidoscope
713-677-7127

Houston
Bo's Place
713-942-8339

Plano
Journey of Hope Grief Support
Center
972-964-1600
www.johgriefsupport.org

San Antonio
Children's Bereavement
Center of South
Texas
210-705-5207

UTAH

Salt Lake City
Bereavement Services,
Primary Children's
Medical Center
801-588-3086

Salt Lake City
The Sharing Place
801-466-6730

VERMONT

Putney
Center for Creative
Healing
802-387-2550

VIRGINIA

Lynchburg
Kids' Haven
804-845-4072

Norfolk
Edmarc
757-668-8600

Richmond
Comfort Zone Camp
804-377-3430
www.comfortzonecamp.org

Roanoke
Camp Treehouse
540-224-4753

Roanoke
Good Samaritan
Hospice
540-776-0198

Resources

WASHINGTON

Bellingham
Camp Willie
360-733-1492

Clarkston
Willow Center
509-758-2902

Longview
Community Home Health &
 Hospice
www.chhh.org

Olympia
SoundCareKids
360-493-5928

Seattle
Rise N Shine
206-628-8949 x227

Tacoma
Bridges
253-403-1837

Vancouver
SW Washington Hospice
360-696-5120

WISCONSIN

Beloit
Beloit Regional Hospice
608-363-7421

Eau Claire
The Healing Place
715-833-6028

Green Bay
Unity Hospice Bereavement
 Services
920-494-0225

Kenosha
MargaretAnn's Place
414-656-9656

Menomonee Falls
When a Parent Dies
414-251-1001

Milwaukee
Bereavement Family Services,
 Children's Hospital
 of Wisconsin
414-266-3325

Photo by Nicole Cappello

Kate Atwood was born and raised in Charlottesville, Virginia. She was twelve when she lost her mother, Audrey Atwood, to breast cancer. Twelve years later, after graduating from the University of Virginia and in the midst of a promising career in sports marketing, she founded Kate's Club. What began as driving a handful of kids around Atlanta to various shows, museums, sports venues and more has now grown into a nationally acclaimed nonprofit organization that has helped hundreds of children and their families deal with the loss of a parent or sibling. As the organization's founder, Kate has been featured on major national media outlets including *People* magazine, CNN and ABC's *The View*. She is continually recognized for her work with these kids and for her philanthropic success at such a young age. Kate has been named by the Turner Broadcasting System as one of its "Pathfinders," featured on CNN as one of its "Young People Who Rock" and hailed by the Atlanta Business Chronicle in its "Top 40 Under 40" feature. She continues to reside in Atlanta and has become a valued resource and sought-after speaker on topics ranging from grief support to social entrepreneurship to community involvement, inspiring others in her generation to give back and more.

John Kelly is a freelance writer based in Charlottesville, Virginia, where he lives with his wife, Angela, and children, Samantha and Christopher. He is regularly published in a variety of magazines including *Albemarle* and the *Arts & Sciences* magazine at the University of Virginia. John is honored to work with the remarkable Kate Atwood on this project and to play even a small role in helping families find hope along the path of one of life's most difficult journeys.